DISCOVERY GUIDES BEST OF

NORTH YORK MOORS & COAST

Contents

COVER PHOTOGRAPHS: (Main Photograph) The famous 'White Horse' near Kilburn;
(Bottom, Left) Runswick Bay; (Bottom, Centre) Commondale Moor; (Bottom, Right) Scarborough Harbour.
Photographs reproduced by kind permission of Discovery Photo Library Ltd.
The maps in this publication are Based upon Ordnance Survey 1 : 25 000 Outdoor Leisure mapping with
the permission of the Controller of Her Majesty's Stationery Office © Crown Copyright

WRITTEN BY MALCOLM PARKER AND CAROLINE HILLERY.
REVISED & EDITED BY EDWARD VENNING. SERIES EDITOR AND DESIGN MALCOLM PARKER.
ARTWORK AND DESIGN ANDREW FALLON & LUCY MADDREN.
PUBLISHED BY DISCOVERY PUBLISHING (UK) LTD., 1 MARKET PLACE,
MIDDLETON-IN-TEESDALE, CO. DURHAM, DL12 0QG. TEL & FAX: (01833) 640638.
PRINTED IN ENGLAND. ISBN 0-86309-180-6. COPYRIGHT DISCOVERY PUBLISHING (UK) LTD.

Introduction to the Area

THE ESSENTIAL ADVANTAGE of the area under consideration in this Guide is that it is really two areas in one! Inland, we have the unspoilt moorland farming landscape, which is protected within the 500 square miles of the **North York Moors National Park.** But along its eastern edge, we also have the dramatic and spectacular cliff coastline, with its rocky headlands and sweeping sandy bays, now protected as **the 'Heritage Coast'.** These two environments, each possessing great variety, offer a contrast of landform, character, wildlife and way of life that can hardly be surpassed anywhere in Britain.

THE MOORS ARE VAST IN EXPANSE, and lonely. Some visitors may even find them intimidating. Others, however, will find their remoteness and massive serenity awesomely beautiful. Whatever your response, it would be wrong to think of the moors as dull or unchanging, for, in addition to the changes of season, there are more subtle changes which literally from hour to hour (according to the time of day or the weather) contribute to an endlessly shifting scene, captivating many visitors and exerting a lasting fascination.

MEANWHILE, IN THE VALLEYS below, lush farmland is punctuated by charming stone-built villages, often clustered around the traditional greens, the whole scene typifying rural England at its best and most unspoilt. This, then, is the character of the North York Moors inland.

ALONG THE COAST, however, it is another story. By contrast with the gently undulating miles of inland countryside, the coast is rugged and dramatic. The **precipitous cliffs** and **rocky headlands** overlook unexpected **sandy bays** and inlets. Anywhere there is access to the sea, a fishing village will be found, squeezed into what space is available, with the houses seemingly piled one on top of another, crowding the narrow lanes. Nothing could be more of a contrast with the comfortable, spreading village greens of the dales settlements. This **coastal world** is a harsher one altogether, a world of storms, sea breezes, the sound of the waves and the wheeling seabirds.

Within these two contrasting environments - the agricultural way of life of the moors and the maritime tradition of the coast - are found a wealth of things to do and places to visit. Let us start with the natural beauties of the region, and consider the many fine landforms and viewpoints which are available to the visitor.

The fine spectacle offered along the coast comes as no surprise, but there are excellent high points and beauty spots inland too. For instance, **Roseberry Topping, Sutton Bank, Ralph Cross** above Rosedale and **Reasty Bank** near Hackness all offer magnificent views. Waterfalls, not enormous but still beautiful, are found too, such as **Mallyan Spout** and **Thomason Foss** near Goathland, and **Falling Foss** near Littlebeck. For more details of all these features, see the chapter on 'Landforms of the Moors'.

HISTORIC ATTRACTIONS are equally numerous and varied, and include both **Bronze Age** burial mounds and **Roman** remains, such as Wade's Causeway near Goathland and Cawthorne Camp near Pickering. But it is with the **Dark Ages** that this region really comes into its own. This little documented period of our history has left us the ancient crosses dotted over the moors, and famous churches of **Saxon** foundation, such as Lastingham Church, St Gregory's Minster near Kirkdale and, of course, Whitby Abbey, whose role in the **establishment of Christianity in England** was so momentous. In 1989, this great ruin celebrated the 450th anniversary of its dissolution under **Henry VIII.**

A brief look at the chapters on **'Castles', 'Abbeys', 'Halls and Gardens',** and **'Museums and Galleries'** of the Area will show what enormous riches there are for the visitor to explore. Every aspect of the region's past is covered, from the farming tradition of the moors to the fishing tradition of the coast, and even the mining and railway developments which belong to the **Industrial Revolution.** Mention of the railways reminds us that this region boasts two of the most scenically appealing routes in the whole of Britain, **the Esk Valley line** from Middlesbrough to Whitby, and **the North York Moors Railway** which links with it at Grosmont and travels down the Newtondale Gorge to Pickering.

There are many other ways to enjoy this remarkable area, not least on foot. Famous long distance walks, such as **the Lyke Wake Walk** or **the Cleveland Way** (featured in a separate chapter) are not by any means the only option. The North York Moors National Park offers leaflets detailing many shorter walks and trails, often examining such special topics as wildlife, geology or industrial archaeology. Please may we urge your support for the Park and the other organisations which exist to protect and maintain the essential character of this very unspoilt and inviting region.

North York Moors National Park

STRIDING ACROSS wild windswept moorland is an unforgettable experience. **Purple heather** beneath the feet and lapwings flying above is, to many, a perfect way to spend a day. To thousands of others, a pleasant drive through a peaceful valley or a gentle stroll along a sandy beach is the makings of a memorable holiday. Never before has the countryside been uppermost in the minds of so many.

The North York Moors is one of eleven National Parks in England and Wales. Within its 553 square miles is one of the finest landscapes in the country - rugged open moorland crossed by deep picturesque dales, a dramatic coastline of cliffs and wykes, and a wealth of wildlife, historic settlements and archaeological remains.

When the **National Parks** were designated, they were charged with preserving the natural beauty of the countryside and promoting the enjoyment of the landscape by the public. Now, almost forty years later, these objectives are as relevant as ever. Changes in farming methods, combined with the desire by more people to experience the wilderness areas of Britain, are bringing increasing pressures on the environment. The 1990s see the National Parks at the forefront in countryside management.

THE NORTH YORK MOORS is a manmade landscape which retains its familiar character through traditional management. For several hundred years sheep, which were first pastured by the monks of **Rievaulx,** have grazed the moorland. However, in the mid C19th, the area became popular for grouse shooting, and management practices deliberately began to encourage the growth of heather. Regular burning or cutting creates a mosaic of young and old plants to provide nutritious green shoots for food and bushier vegetation to protect the nests. Unlike **pheasant** and **partridge,** the **red grouse,** which is unique to Britain, cannot be bred in captivity. Only by managing the moorland to provide an ideal habitat do the grouse numbers remain high. Today, the moorland of the North York Moors forms the largest continuous tract of heather in England and Wales, and provides a home for many upland breeding birds. It is the management of the moorland for grouse and sheep that ensures its continued survival by providing a vital contribution to the local economy.

Although most of the moorland is privately owned, the National Park has a responsibility towards its well-being. A number of schemes have been set up to enable the Park Department and landowners to work together to manage the moorland. One of the main problems is the alarming rate at which bracken is encroaching on the moor. The dense shade cast by the fronds prevents the growth of heather and other plants, so grants are available to farmers to spray the bracken in an attempt to control its spread. Assistance is also given for heather cutting to provide suitable conditions for grouse and to retain the character of the Park.

FARMING IS THE MAJOR ACTIVITY in the North York Moors, and the landscape patterns which we see today are the result of an active farming community. The **dales and moors** have been farmed for hundreds of years, but changes in technology and economic pressures on hill farmers threaten to alter this much loved landscape. Again the National Park has developed its role in **supporting the local people.** Only by maintaining a viable farming community can we hope to retain our unspoilt views and rich patchwork of fields. Farmers can call upon National Park staff to advise them on the best way of managing their land for conservation. Financial help is available to preserve the **herb-rich meadows,** the **dry stone walls** so valuable to the appearance of the landscape, and the **woodlands and copses** so vital to the wildlife of the area.

BUILDINGS also contribute to the aesthetic value of the countryside, and through planning controls the Authority seeks to retain the landscape quality for which the National Park was designated. Owners are encouraged to repair their properties using **traditional methods** and materials so that the very special character of the villages and farms can be maintained.

THE NATIONAL PARK is here to be enjoyed and discovered. Many walks and trails have been developed to encourage people to explore the countryside. **The Visitor Centres at Danby and Sutton Bank** provide the opportunity for visitors to learn more about the National Park, its role, and the work of its officers. At both centres you will find National Park publications explaining the history and **way of life of the area,** as well as details of guided walks, village shows and special events.

The **landscape** of the National Park has been greatly influenced through the centuries by man. Today the aim is not to prevent change but to control it in such a way that the beauty and interest are maintained, not only for ourselves but for future generations.

Early Settlers

The area of the **North York Moors and Coast** has a great variety of landscape and environment in which man has settled and established his existence. Today, **an intricate pattern of land-use and settlement** can be seen which has evolved over the many thousands of years it has taken to forge the identity of the people of this part of North Yorkshire.

THE EARLIEST EVIDENCE OF HUMAN ACTIVITY in the area is the collection of **Mesolithic** (Middle Stone Age) flints that have been discovered, dating from circa 7000 BC. It is believed that these people were nomadic wanderers, and that it was not until much later, in the **Neolithic Age** (New Stone Age), that permanent settlement commenced. Some of the earliest dwellings identified were pile-houses, built on the shores of the lake which once filled the **Vale of Pickering.**

By the beginning of the **Bronze Age**, circa 1800 BC, permanent settlement was becoming more established, and it is from this period that the first substantial archaeological finds date. Excavation has revealed fragments of bowls and cups, small items including beads of **Whitby jet,** and urns filled with charred bones. A large number of tumuli or burial mounds have been investigated, including **Shunner Howe, Sil Howe** and **Loose Howe,** where a fully-clothed male body with a dagger was discovered laid in a coffin - or possibly a dug-out canoe - hewn from an oak tree. These **burial mounds** are nearly always situated in locations with good views. This was clearly of importance when siting a grave, but we do not know enough to understand why.

IT WAS PROBABLY THE BRONZE AGE PEOPLE who built many of the **stone circles** that are found throughout the moors. None of these are spectacular but they are sited in conspicuous positions, such as **Danby Rigg, Bridestones** and **Blakey Topping.** Another feature which has been attributed to these people is the number of dykes or ditches which have a parallel ridge. Their exact purpose is still uncertain. One suggestion is that they were for defensive purposes - although it is difficult to understand what was being defended! Another suggestion is that they were **tribal boundaries** or **animal enclosures.** However, until more substantial evidence is forthcoming, one can only speculate as to their function. There are other puzzling remains from this earliest period of man's occupation. On lonely, windswept sites on the moors, we find single standing stones and stone cairns. The purpose of both is unknown.

Good examples of Bronze Age remains are found at **Studford Ring** (a hill above Ampleforth), **Farndale, Blakey Ridge** and **Bilsdale East Moor.** In some of these, flint chippings were found in such large quantities that the existence of a whole community, based on the manufacture of flint tools, seems likely.

Another impressive site is Park Pale, a two mile long rampart on the moor above the village of **Commondale.** With only antler picks as tools, this represents an engineering feat of some magnitude - and we can only guess at the thousands of man-hours that must have been worked to achieve such a construction.

The Bronze Age also marked the start of the **clearance of the forests** of oak, birch, elm and hazel, which covered much of the area and which have eventually been replaced by the expanse of **heather moorland** we see today. Indeed, the enigmatic stone cairns mentioned earlier may be nothing more than another facet of this huge labour of clearance. What we do know is that **the population of the moors,** both man and animal, was higher in the Bronze Age than at any time before or since, a remarkable fact which helps us to understand how a primitive people could have had such a dramatic impact on our area.

LARGE NUMBERS OF PEOPLE, however, do not necessarily mean a settled civilisation. Even with the coming of **the Iron Age,** several hundred years BC, there was still no organised settlement of the area, and wild tribes, surviving chiefly as hunter-gatherers, were still roaming the region.

Such settlements as there were would have been of a relatively temporary nature, with small groups clearing an area of trees in order to form **enclosures** for their few animals, most usually goats, and to grow crops, which would have consisted of wheat and barley. **The thinness of the topsoil** would have made it necessary to move on fairly regularly in order to eke out a living and, in any case, there was almost certainly the problem of harassment by **neighbouring tribes,** making it difficult to remain settled. Certainly, the tribesmen of the area were considered particularly bellicose by the next people to arrive, who were **the Romans.** The fiercest of all received the Roman name 'Brigantes', the origin of our word 'brigand'. For all their ferocity, however, they were never a match for the disciplined might of their Roman conquerors.

The Romans

THE ROMAN CONQUEST took place in the years following AD 71, the date of the establishment of **Eboracum (York)**, which gave the Romans a base from which to set about subduing the wild tribesmen to the North. We know that in AD 80, **the Ninth Legion** was dispatched with this end in view, to bring the Brigantes under control.

There are many features which serve to show the presence of the Romans in the area, the main ones being **Cawthorne Camps** and **Wade's Causeway.** However, until recently, with the emergence of new evidence proving a more extensive occupation, there was very little to show that there had been any more than minimal Roman settlement. Scattered finds include coins, pottery shards, beads and one bronze helmet, but we have to wait until around AD 400 to find substantial remains.

THE ROMANS ESTABLISHED FORTS at **Malton** and **York** and, probably during the latter period of their occupation, a series of coastal signal stations as an early warning system against sea-borne attack. **Malton** was the site of a fortified town named **Derventio**, and this was surrounded by a civilian settlement which would have grown up to supply the needs of the soldiers. **Malton Museum,** now housed in the old Town Hall, displays the large number of interesting finds from this site.

Cawthorne Camps, located near Cropton, a few miles north of Pickering, consist of four earthen ramparts and ditches and were probably occupied for only a short time following their rapid construction circa AD 110. This encampment may have served as a **training ground for soldiers** from the garrisons at Malton and York. It seems that trainee soldiers may have used this area for practice in the **construction of military camp sites,** as some of the layouts appear to be experimental and incomplete.

Linking the camps, probably to another small camp on Lease Rigg which overlooks Grosmont in the Esk Valley, was **Wade's Causeway.** This **Roman road,** built circa AD 80, is now thought to have run all the way from the coastal signal stations through Cawthorne to Malton and thence to York, and is in fact **the only road known** to have reached into the vast wilderness of North East Yorkshire. It is the best-preserved stretch of Roman road in the country and can be seen on **Wheeldale Moor,** about 3 miles south-west of Goathland.

IMMEDIATELY AFTER THE ROMANS departed from the area, the road began to be ripped up for re-use in buildings - and this process was still continuing centuries later. For instance, the stone came in particularly useful for walling during the **Acts of Enclosure** in the C18th. Even to this day, unprotected stretches are still being destroyed, but the present protected length is safe, thanks to the efforts of the late James Patterson of Wheeldale Lodge, **gamekeeper to the Duchy of Lancaster.** In the first twenty years of this century, he uncovered 1.25 miles of the road. Formed from massive flagstones, and with its side gutters and culverts still in place, it is in a remarkably complete state. The labour of laying it was probably carried out by the newly-conquered local people, working more or less as slaves for the Roman soldiers.

From **Derventio,** another road is now known to have travelled east to what today is **Scarborough.** Here there was **a coastal signal station** surveying the North Sea. This was part of a larger network, and remains of other signal stations have been found at **Filey,** near **Robin Hood's Bay, Whitby** and **Saltburn.**

Finally, remains of two **Roman villas** have been discovered, one at **Hovingham** and the other to the east of **Helmsley.** All in all, evidence is mounting to show that Roman occupation of our area was more extensive than was originally thought, and no doubt more remains to be found. Even so, it would have to be conceded that there is nothing here to compare with the marvels of **Hadrian's Wall** and its associated camps or, for that matter, with Roman remains to be found in the south.

IT ALWAYS SEEMS INCREDIBLE that the obvious benefits of Roman civilisation - the homes enjoying sophisticated plumbing and heating systems, or the efficient communications via the road networks and signalling stations, to name but two - should have been largely lost so soon **after the Roman withdrawal.** The fact is that the Romans kept themselves apart, employing local people to supply their needs but not absorbing them into the Roman way of life. This failure to integrate meant that when the Romans went, most of their efficient and organised lifestyle went with them. **Local people** might use the beautifully cut stones from their buildings and roads, but the intricacies of street drainage or under-floor heating, and certainly the niceties of bath-houses and latrines, were beyond them. It was all too easy to step backwards into what we now term **the Dark Ages.**

The Dark Ages

The next people to arrive, many via the Humber Estuary, were the **Saxons**, towards the end of the C3rd. For a time the invaders were mostly repulsed, the efficiency of the Roman signal stations on the coast being a factor but, around AD 410, the decree came from Rome ordering the withdrawal of forces from Britain to defend the Roman Empire's territories in the Eastern Mediterranean. This left **the native Britons** to face the fearsome new invaders on their own - and fearsome they certainly were. Part of a Roman coastguard fort was found at Huntcliff (the rest having been washed into the sea) and here the remains of fourteen men, women and children were found at the bottom of the well, presumably massacred by the invaders.

THE ANGLO-SAXONS, as we now know them, eventually controlled large areas of the North of England. These they divided into kingdoms, the largest of which was **Northumbria**, which stretched from the Humber to the Forth. This they then sub-divided into two regions: Bernicia to the north and Deira to the south.

The **capital** of this latter **kingdom of Deira** was **Streonshalh**, which we now know as **Whitby**. Saxon settlements can still be identified today by studying the place names. For example any settlement ending in '-ton' is likely to be Saxon, such as Carlton, Thornton, Wrelton, Brompton, Lockton, Newton and Sinnington... with the largest concentration being to the south of the area. Many other words, such as 'dale', 'gill', 'beck', 'thorpe' and 'gate' (meaning 'street') also have their origins in this period.

Later, towards the end of the C8th, the **Scandinavians**, especially **the Danes**, began to arrive ... at first to raid and destroy; then later to build and live alongside the **Anglo-Saxons**. Tradition has it that **King Arthur** and his knights won a famous battle against them at Eston Nab. If so, the victory was short-lived and the invasions continued. It was not until around AD 927 that the conflict between Saxons and Danes was resolved and the country was united under one sovereign. **Danish settlements** in the area are concentrated in the north-west (Swainby, Ingleby and Boltby) and along the east coast (Whitby, Scalby, Mickleby and Boulby). The place name ending '-by' is indicative of a Scandinavian origin, and it was the Danes who **divided Yorkshire into its three 'Ridings'.**

Despite this long period of unrest, however, these centuries had also seen the establishment of **Christianity** in the area. In AD 596 **Pope Gregory** had instructed **St Augustine** to undertake the conversion of the Anglo-Saxons. His delegate to Northumbria was **Paulinus,** who managed to convert the local ruler, **Edwin.** Thus began a tradition of Christian kings in Northumbria, among whom one significant figure was **King Oswy.** In AD 657 he fought the pagan **King Penda** at the **Battle of Widwinfield.** Before the battle, he promised, in return for victory, to devote his daughter, **Lady Hilda,** then 44 years old, to the Lord as a holy virgin and to provide her with land for the foundation of a monastery. Victory was his, with the resulting building of the monastery of **Streonshalh,** the earliest in our area, which developed into Whitby Abbey. In AD 664, it became famous as the location of **the Synod of Whitby,** which was called by King Oswy to reconcile the differences between the **Roman and Celtic churches.** The major problem was over the date of Easter, with the eventual ruling being made in favour of Rome, represented by **Wilfrid.**

A SECOND INFLUENCE CAME from the Irish church, established on Lindisfarne in AD 634 by **St Aidan.** By AD 687 his successor, **St Cuthbert,** had died and, harassed by the pagan Norsemen, the **monks of Lindisfarne** were forced to leave the island, and spent many subsequent years travelling the North-East of England with the coffin of the saint. As is well-known, they eventually found a resting-place at Durham, and our most perfect Norman cathedral is the result. One stopping place during their years of wandering was probably **Kirkleatham,** where the present church is dedicated to St Cuthbert and contains a child's coffin of very early date. The tiny church of **Upleatham** also contains a relic of the same period, part of an Anglo-Danish cross. This fascinating and turbulent period of local history can be explored 'on the ground' by visiting some of the region's abbeys.

THE ANCIENT STONE CROSSES which stand on the moors, marking junctions and meeting places as well as sites of religious significance, also belong to this period of early Christianity. The oldest still in existence is 'Lilla', near Fylingdales, supposedly erected in honour of Lilla, who gave his own life to save the C7th King Edwin. Others that can still be found are **Mauley's Cross** at the start of the Newtondale Forest Drive, 'Fat Betty' at the head of Rosedale and, not far away, 'Old Ralph' and 'Young Ralph'. This last is of much later date, probably belonging to the C13th, and is the one which has been adopted as the symbol of the National Park.

After the Norman Conquest

THE 'DARK AGES' CAME TO AN END with the arrival of the final newcomers, the Normans, who invaded under **William the Conqueror** in 1066. Our area played its own part in that story because William's conquest was made easier by the state of the British army under **King Harold at Hastings.** The reason for this was that Harold's forces had, only shortly before, marched north to fight the invading Danish King, Harald Hardrada of Norway. Though victorious, they immediately had to march south again to face William.

There was a **period of unrest** following the Norman invasion, only resolved by a savage visit from William himself, in 1069, when the whole of this area was laid waste: an ugly episode known as 'The Harrying of the North'. We have dramatic accounts of the battle fought near Redcar in which the northern earls, led by Edwin and Morcar, were defeated. The **Domesday Book** of 1086 provides valuable knowledge of life at this period. It lists most of the local manors as 'waste' and shows that settlement was restricted to the coastal fringe and the lower slopes. It was only with a growing population in subsequent centuries that settlement extended back into the moorlands and upper valleys, which at this period had become almost completely depopulated.

THE PRESENCE OF THE NORMANS is clearly evident in the large number of castles and monasteries, many still visible today. The castles, built to enforce the complete subjugation of the remaining people, stand as testimony to the power of the Norman barons. Meanwhile, **the huge Norman monasteries** indicate the comparable power and influence of the monks who, incidentally, were responsible for the introduction of sheep farming into the area, an occupation which is still of great economic importance today. They also initiated huge ridge and furrow drainage systems to render the wetlands more useful, and had iron foundries, salt pans, fisheries, and extensive mining interests. Eventually they were combining the peaceful, contemplative life with one of extreme prosperity - and this very prosperity was to cause their downfall.

In the mid 1530s, **Henry VIII,** having declared himself head of the English church in direct opposition to the Pope, ordered the dissolution of the monasteries, and set about rewarding his more intractable barons by distributing the monastic estates among them.

The beautiful but tragic ruins of **Byland, Rievaulx** and **Whitby Abbeys,** and **Guisborough** and **Mount Grace Priories,** are some of those which bear witness to this period. The pattern of social and agricultural development that we see today stems from this early example of privatisation!

The **quarrel with the Pope** had some advantages, however. For instance, the production of alum, used as a fixative for the popular Turkey Red dyes, had hitherto been a papal monopoly. Henry's destruction of that monopoly allowed **the development of the alum industry** on the coast from Ravenscar northwards, an industry which survives even today. But many problems were created by the dissolution of the monasteries, not least the loss of their function as providers of education, only made good with the foundation of universities as an alternative source of learning.

DURING THE MIDDLE AGES, therefore, the ordinary people of the area fell broadly into two main categories, those on the coast engaged in fishing and those inland working as agricultural labourers under the **Feudal System.** Power struggles between **feudal lords** and the **Norman kings** were constant and skirmishes were common. Numerous local castles, some not much more than fortified houses, were built as a result - but many of them were constructed mainly of wood so that their sites, of **motte and bailey** outline, are all that remain, sometimes with buildings of much later date atop them. The most impressive remains of the Norman era can be seen in the ruins of Helmsley, Pickering and Scarborough Castles.

DURING THE ENGLISH CIVIL WAR of 1642 to 1649, battles were fought in the area between **Roundheads** and **Cavaliers.** Sieges took place at Scarborough and Helmsley Castles. Scarborough was held for Parliament by Sir Hugh Cholmley, but he later declared for the King, and a siege ensued which lasted from February 1644 until July 1645, with the defenders eventually capitulating in a very depleted condition. Three years later, a second siege took place but was resolved much more rapidly, again in favour of **the Parliamentarians.** Sir Gordon Crosland was in charge of Helmsley Castle when it was also besieged in 1644 by 1000 troops led by Sir Thomas Fairfax, and held out three months before surrendering.

A more peaceful period, and one which would see great changes and increased prosperity, was now at hand.

Recent Centuries

THE MAJOR AGRICULTURAL CHANGE during the C18th and C19th was due to **the Acts of Enclosure,** which divided previously 'common' land into strips and allocated these in theoretically fair amounts to local farmers. In practice, the wealthier the farmer the larger his allocation, so that many small farms had to be sold to save their owners from ruin. **Sheep farming** remained the most important source of income. Paved causeways or **'drovers' roads'** now networked the region, with local merchants travelling huge distances to sell their goods. Cattle, sheep, pigs and geese, frequently shod like horses, or in the case of the geese with their feet dipped in tar to protect them, were driven mile after mile to whatever was considered the most advantageous selling place, some coming from as far north as Scotland. **Packhorses** also carried wool, salt, dried fish and other goods to market. These many travellers needed accommodation, of course, and local inns did a good trade, with the visitors being particularly welcome for the news they brought of the world outside.

This hitherto remote community, however, was soon to enjoy communications of a quite different order. The coming of **the Industrial Revolution** within the C19th brought unprecedented changes to our area. We have already seen the beginnings of the alum industry on the coast, and the Cleveland area now found sudden prosperity as an important **ironstone mining** centre. This resulted in the rapid development of a **local railway system,** initiated by **George Stephenson's** enterprising rail line through Newtondale to Whitby, which in turn led to increased trade for many of the local fishing communities.

The Victorian entrepreneur, **George Hudson,** was eventually able to transport mill-workers from the West Riding to the now flourishing coastal towns of Scarborough and Bridlington by rail. The improved facilities for travel also brought the first large numbers of tourists, and elegant Victorian spa resorts, such as Scarborough and Saltburn, were quick to build on their good fortune in having mineral waters considered beneficial to health.

THE EARLY WARNING ARRANGEMENTS, first established along the coast as signal stations in Roman times, had been preserved as a beacon signalling system and had a serious role to play throughout the period. During the Elizabethan age it had been feared that the **Spanish Armada** would attack, coming round the northern tip of Scotland, and in the C19th lookouts anxiously scanned the sea for fear of invasion from **Napoleonic France,** again via the northern route. This early form of communication was very simple. One light would mean that ships were sighted, two lights would indicate that there were invasion ships and three lights would indicate that a landing was imminent and that people should evacuate inland.

Apart from a bizarre episode in 1779, when an **American buccaneer** of British origin, called **Paul Jones,** made an alarming but futile naval attack at Skinningrove, no invasion ever came. Indeed, the lookout posts were far more occupied with trying to apprehend smugglers, who made constant use of the many coves and inlets along the coast!

In the twentieth century, on the 16th of December 1914, the coastal towns did face an actual attack. **Three German battle cruisers,** the Blucher, Moltke and Siedlitz, unleashed a bombardment of high explosive shells, destroying **six hundred houses** in Hartlepool alone and causing many deaths. Scarborough Castle was also badly damaged. Later, the surveying of the North Sea and the airspace above was done in a more sophisticated way, using the famous radar-scanning white spheres of **Fylingdales Moor,** once called the three golf balls - a monstrous intrusion in the countryside. Fortunately, they were recently dismantled and replaced by a single receiver shaped like a steeply pitched roof and referred to locally as **'the pyramid'.**

A recent link between present and past came in 1977 during the **Silver Jubilee Celebrations.** The beacon system transmitted its message from Windsor to Ben Nevis, the Orkney Islands and Shetland Islands in the far north. Some of the most ancient beacon points can still be identified in this area at such places as **Danby Beacon** above Eskdale and **Roseberry Topping** near Great Ayton.

THE PEOPLE OF THE MOORS and coast today display a tenacity, a sincerity and a humour that is the result of years of evolution. Not only have they inherited the **qualities of their ancestors,** but their taming of and coming to terms with the environment in which they live, whether it be the bleakness of the wild moorlands or the relentless power and sudden cruelty of the sea, has bred into them a **firm independence** and **strength of character.** A general background has been provided, but there is much more to discover.

Famous People

There are many famous people who have either lived in or have an association with this area. To select individuals to describe here is obviously an almost impossible task, but various names do come to mind. First and foremost, of course, we think of **Captain James Cook** (1728-1779), by far the most internationally known, whose connections with this area are explained elsewhere.

His contemporary was the writer **Laurence Sterne** (1713-1768). Like many a penniless young man, Sterne sought a career in the church, obtaining his first parish in 1738 at Sutton-on-the-Forest. Three years later he married Miss Elizabeth Lumley but he was not a faithful husband and his unfortunate wife went insane in 1759 - driven to it, many people said, by his philandering. The following year he began 'Tristram Shandy', which eventually ran to nine volumes, almost entirely made up of whimsical digressions, and using a host of eccentric characters. It was widely denounced at the time by **Dr Johnson** and many others, on moral as well as literary grounds. Sterne, in 1760, became curate of Coxwold and moved into the house he named 'Shandy Hall', now a museum to his memory. Ill-health took him to France in 1762, and in 1765 he undertook a seven months' tour of France and Italy, which provided him with the material for his 'A Sentimental Journey'. He died in poverty in 1768.

Although not of local origin, **Canon Atkinson** MA DCL, lived and worked in this area for over half a century. Born in 1814, in Essex, he was ordained in 1841 and took up a curacy at Scarborough. He became vicar of Danby in the Esk Valley in 1847, where he remained until his death in 1900.

AN ACUTE OBSERVER with a keen interest in his surroundings, Atkinson soon became aware of the depth and subtleties of the local dialect through the regular contact with local people that was demanded by his ministry. His collection of words, expressions and pronunciations was published in 1868, as 'A Glossary of the Cleveland Dialect'. This monumental work established his fame as a historian and remains to this day the only comprehensive work of its kind on the area. Encouraged by many, including the publisher George MacMillan, Atkinson enjoyed huge success with publication in 1891 of his best known work, 'Forty Years in a Moorland Parish'.

Subtitled 'Reminiscences and Researches in Danby and Cleveland', the book contains chapters on folklore and customs, history, archaeology and geology, as well as notes on natural history. In the preface to the first edition, Atkinson records that he 'must have walked more than **70,000 miles** in the prosecution of his clerical work alone; and much more than as many again for exercise, relaxation or recreation'. During his long lifetime at Danby, he published many notable works, among them 'History of Cleveland', 'British Birds', 'Eggs and Nests', 'Walks, Talks and Travels','Ancient Whitby and its Abbey' and 'The Last of the Giant Killers'.

In the early C19th another notable local figure was **John Costello** (or Castillo), known as the **Bard of the Dales.** He was a stonemason and poet who grew up in Eskdale. His poems, in local dialect, were well known, and he also became a celebrated Methodist preacher. At the end of the century, **Bram Stoker,** the author of 'Dracula', stayed for a time in Whitby. Also living in Whitby at that time was the gifted early photographer, **Frank Meadow Sutcliffe,** now famous as a result of the rediscovery and publication of his albums portraying life among the fishing community of Whitby at the turn of the century.

The members of the gifted and eccentric **Sitwell family** regularly visited their grandmother, Lady Louisa Sitwell, at Wood End, her house in Scarborough, and later lived there themselves for long periods. The house is now home to the **Wood End Museum,** and two rooms are devoted to the Sitwells and their literary works. Osbert, in particular, gives us amusing recollections of life at Wood End in his autobiography, recalling how 'the frequent storms gave, indeed, an awful vivid excitement to life in winter'. Finally, the best-known names from our own day are those of James Herriot and **Alan Ayckbourn,** the Scarborough-based playwright.

These, then, are just a few famous people associated with our area. Mention could be made of **George Stephenson** and **George Hudson,** who did so much to develop the railway from Pickering to Whitby, **George Cayley of Brompton,** a pioneer of aviation and **William Marshall of Pickering,** the pioneer of agricultural education. Famous visitors included the author **Charles Dickens,** the poet **Wordsworth** and the artist **Cotman,** not to mention practically every king of England since the Norman Conquest who came to Pickering Castle for the hunting - all impressed by this area and leaving their impressions on it.

*Myths &
Legends*

All parts of the country have their own **legends** and **superstitions**, often so embedded in the fabric of everyday life that they become reality itself! The North York Moors and Coast are well-endowed with interesting stories from two distinctive communities, the farmers of the countryside and the fishermen of the coast. Therefore, we are spoilt for choice ... which tales do we include?

SOME OF THE OLDEST and most amusing concern the **two Cleveland Giants, Wade** and his wife **Bel**. He is said to have built Wade's Causeway for her convenience when driving her cattle to pasture; but in less amiable mood scooped up and threw a mighty clod of earth at her, thereby creating both the Hole of Horcum and Blakey Topping! Together, they are held to have built Helmsley and Pickering Castles, chucking a great hammer to and fro across the 20 mile distance between!

Perhaps my favourite story is told by **Bram Stoker,** who stayed at Whitby in the late 1890s whilst completing part of his world-famous novel, **'Dracula'.** It tells how Count Dracula was involved in a shipwreck in a violent storm off Whitby and, taking the form of a large dog, rushed up **the 199 steps** from the harbour to St Mary's Church, next to Whitby Abbey, and sought refuge in the grave of a suicide victim. Today, in the churchyard can be found a gravestone **bearing a skull and crossbones** - is this really the grave of a pirate or is it something far more sinister and terrifying? Having stood in the graveyard at midnight with only the deafening blow of the wind for company and a full moon for light, I can tell you, from experience, of the electric charge to the atmosphere, **the heightening of the senses** and the tingling in one's nerves and sinews. How many of you dare come here completely alone on a stormy winter's night, such as the one of the shipwreck, and stand in the full moon and be able to say that Dracula does not exist? Remember, when you hear the unearthly, blood-chilling howl of **the evil hound** ... it will be too late for you to change your mind!

Perhaps the most common of country tales are those of hobs, or **hobgoblins,** elf-like creatures which many older country-folk still believe actually exist! These hobs fall into two main categories, the mischievous and the helpful; and both types are found in abundance in this area, including **T'Hob of Broxa, T'Hob of Tarn Hole** and the **Hob Hole Hob of Runswick** who could cure whooping cough. One well-known tale concerns a mischievous hob who was forever pestering a local farmer and making his life impossible. This farmer lived in West Gill, a small tributary valley off Farndale. So desperate he became at being unable to get any peace, he decided to move out of the area. Loading his cart with his possessions, he set off but had not gone far when he met a neighbour who greeted him with 'Ah see thou's flittin' - to which the hob, who had hidden on the cart, replied, 'Aye, we's flittin'. The farmer, resigned to his fate of never being rid of his tormentor, turned the cart around and said in exasperation, 'Well if thou's flittin too, we might as well gan yam ageean' and they set off back to West Gill.

OTHER LEGENDS have a less humorous ending. One of these is about **Sarkless Kitty of Farndale.** In 1787, the young and beautiful Kitty Garthwaite was deeply in love with Willie Dixon of Hutton. To see as much of him as possible, she would wait at the alder tree beside the ford over the **River Dove at Lowna.** One evening he did not arrive. So upset was Kitty at her apparently unrequited love that she drowned herself in the deep pool beside the ford. The next day her body was found, clad only in a white sark. She was taken to the nearby mill and laid at rest while her sark was removed, washed and hung up to dry. Two days later, Willie Dixon returned, having been secretly to obtain a special licence to marry Kitty, only to be greeted with the tragic news. However, **Kitty's body and her sark had disappeared.** That night, in his despair, Willie ventured to the ford, where he met and was entranced by Kitty who led him to his death in the deep pool that had claimed her. So bitter was she, that her revenge was to provide the same fate to all men. Every year, upon the anniversary of her death, the body of a young man would be found in the pool. The apparition of the beautiful naked body of Kitty carrying her sark would strike terror into all the menfolk of the area. Eventually **the vicar of Lastingham** was persuaded to perform a proper burial service beside the pool and, since this time, no more young men have been enticed to their deaths. But beware the beautiful apparition of **Sarkless Kitty of Farndale;** perhaps her tormented spirit is not yet fully at rest.

FINALLY, Goathland and Egton Bridge share a tragic legend of **the wicked Lord Julian and the Spinning Maiden** who haunted him for his cruelty to her. When he died, the area became terrorised by **a monstrous 'Gytrash',** and it was not until the local people arranged a confrontation between the two apparitions that the evil chain of events was broken.

Traditional Crafts

IN TODAY'S WORLD of mass production and synthetic materials, it is all too easy for us to lose sight of the fact that in the past, local people had to manufacture almost all their requirements themselves from natural materials that were readily to hand. Poor roads also restricted the distribution of both raw materials and the finished products, so local industries developed to serve the surrounding community.

With the coming of the Industrial Revolution in C19th and improvements in communication, many of these **crafts** began to decline. Some died out completely, while others, like the **knitting of fishermen's 'gansey's'** (jerseys) at Staithes, remained in the remoter parts of the country. Each settlement used to have its own pattern of gansey, knitted in five ply wool on five needles, and some of these will still be found in the villages to which they belong.

An old thatched cottage at Ryedale Folk Museum

The area is perhaps most famous for its ancient craft of **woodcarving.** The best known workshop is probably that established early this century by Robert Thompson, **the 'Mouseman' of Kilburn.** Some of his work can be seen in the church at Castleton in the Esk Valley, carved with the mice that he always hid on his work, which gave him his nickname.

However, the animal that has made the largest impact in the last quarter century has been **the beaver.** This is the trademark of **Colin Almack,** who specialised in domestic furniture. His work is still carried on by his family in his workshop, Beaver Lodge, at **Sutton-under-Whitestonecliffe,** which is open to visitors. Specialising mainly in English oak they have developed an excellent reputation and are undertaking an increasing amount of work for churches. Recent customers have been Southwark Cathedral and Eton College. Other animal trademarks in woodcarving are the **squirrel,** the fox-head, and the wren of **Bob Hunter,** another excellent craftsman who has a well-stocked showroom in the rural village of **Thirlby.** These are a few of the woodcarvers and cabinet-makers of the area.

If you are after something durable and elegant for the garden, however, look no further than **Forge Products** located at Hutton-le-Hole, with their appealing **outdoor furniture.** Then, if you need somewhere beautiful to put your newly acquired garden seat, why not take the opportunity to brush up on another craft to be found in the area: **gardening.** When we think of crafts, we usually think automatically of articles made from wood, clay, glass, wool, enamels - all 'dead' media. Yet gardening also creates beauty, this time from a living form, and since the end of the C19th, when a huge range of exotic plants began to pour into Great Britain, many of us have become keen gardeners.

POET'S COTTAGE SHRUB NURSERY at Lealholm is a particularly attractive garden centre, with its own landscaped nursery garden, and historic association with **John Castillo, the 'Bard of the Dales',** who lived here over a hundred years ago. It was started in 1978 by **Hilda Rees** and her late husband as a result of visitors asking to look round what was originally their private garden.

Another craft, one of great antiquity, whose practitioners have traditionally been given pride of place in the craft community, was the working of iron into the tools and goods essential to farmers. In many villages, **the blacksmith** would have been the most important person after the priest, and although much of the old business of the rural blacksmith disappeared with the coming of the motorcar, some of the practitioners of this craft have adapted. For example, **Phoenix Forge** is well-known for its commissioned ironwork.

Mention must also be made of the flourishing **potteries** in the area, but we must not forget the **glass workshops** such as the very popular **Whitby Glass Studios,** makers of the famous Whitby Lucky Ducks, and stockists of a wide range of other attractive ornaments.

The Geology of the Area

THE OLDEST ROCKS exposed in our area are the dark grey shales, with occasional thin layers of ironstone, which are to be found in the deep moorland valleys and along the western and northern escarpments of the moors. These rocks, collectively known as **the Lias Series**, belong to **the Lower Jurassic Period** and are approximately 180 million years old. They were originally laid down as fine silts and muds on the floor of a deep sea that extended over a large part of what is now Yorkshire.

During the late C19th and early C20th, many **mines** were opened to exploit these **ironstones**, particularly in the northern areas of the Park. In **Rosedale**, for instance, the old tips, kilns and railway track beds are still very clearly seen; and **Roseberry Topping**, near Great Ayton, owes its craggy face to mining activity.

THE DEEP-WATER, MARINE CONDITIONS of the Lias Period eventually gave way to the shallow, fresh-water conditions of **a huge delta**, where vast quantities of sand and mud accumulated and were compressed, forming over 150 metres (500 feet) of **sandstone** and **mudstone**. It is these rocks which today form the backbone of the North York Moors, and outcrop as the conspicuous 'edges' frequented by rock climbers. The majority of the older houses in the northern areas of the Park are constructed from the local sandstone.

As conditions gradually changed once again, **the delta** was invaded by the sea for the last time. The group of rocks which formed over the next few million years are all of marine origin, as a close study of their fossil content will prove. This series **(the Middle Oolites)** consists of layers of sandstones, clays and limestones which today form **the Hambleton and Tabular Hills**, extending from Sutton Bank in the west to Scarborough in the east. To the south, the rocks disappear under the **Vale of Pickering**, but gradually rise in the north and terminate in an impressive north facing escarpment overlooking the high moorlands. A representative example of the local limestone can be seen at **Roulston Scar**, where the naturally greyish-cream colouring is exposed.

Following the deposition of the Middle Oolites, the sea once again deepened and the **Kimmeridge clay**, such as covers the fertile Vale of Pickering, was formed. The end of this period brings us to a time around 130 million years ago. Little is known of the subsequent **Cretaceous Period**, whose best known rocks are the white chalk deposits seen in **the Yorkshire Wolds** and **Flamborough Head**. But we do know that some 60 to 70 million years ago our area was uplifted, and processes of erosion began to mould the landscape into its present form.

FROM THE TERTIARY PERIOD, 58 million years ago, dates the one intrusion, when a stream of molten lava formed **the Cleveland Dyke**, also known as the Whinstone Ridge. This hard, volcanic rock, found in a narrow band from Sneaton High Moor to Great Ayton, was at one time quarried for road-surfacing material.

A more recent event which has moulded our landscape was the Great or **Quaternary Ice Age** which began some one million years ago and ended about 10,000 years ago. During this period it is uncertain whether **ice** covered the high moors but evidence suggests vast ice sheets on three sides of our area. These blocked the streams which had previously flowed west to the vale of York or east to the sea, **forming huge glacial lakes** in the moorland valleys.

When the ice later melted, with raging meltwater flowing from one valley to the next, **channels** were cut into the hillsides which can still be seen today. The water eventually escaped south into **Lake Pickering** by cutting two valleys which are among the most dramatic and picturesque in the National Park, the **Newtondale Gorge** and the **Forge Valley** near Hackness. Meanwhile, to the north west, distinctive steep-sided hills like **Roseberry Topping** and **Cringle Moor** stood proud of the ice sheet and were moulded to their present form by the force of the meltwaters flowing round their flanks.

A fascinating indication of the **tundra-type wildlife** of the glacial period came in 1821, when John Gibson, on holiday in Helmsley, found the **Kirkdale Cave**, containing the remains of some 200 hyenas and their kills; these included hippopotamus, woolly rhinoceros, bison, wild ox, straight-tusked elephant, mammoth, lion and others, most previously unknown in England, and dated to around 70,000 BC.

GEOLOGY ENTHUSIASTS will enjoy the **Ravenscar Geological Trail**, where a major fault has exposed successive layers of rock that would normally be deep underground. There are two parts to the trail, an easy first section of two and a half miles, followed by a more taxing stretch of two miles. Here, the panoramic views along the coast provides a good reminder of how nature's forces continue to mould and shape the land.

Rocks &
Fossils

IT IS THE GEOLOGY OF THE AREA that controls and is responsible for the shape and altitude of its landscape. Each particular **rock type** has its own characteristics and reacts differently to **weathering** and the agents of **erosion.** In general, harder, more resistant rocks produce high prominent landscapes, whereas softer, less resistant rocks produce lower and flatter landscapes.

Although the deposits found along the North Yorkshire coast are restricted to the **Jurassic Period,** and to a lesser extent, the **Quaternary Ice Age** one million years ago, there is still a great variety of rock types which provide equally varied landforms and scenery. As a result, this coastline has proved very popular with geologists, including **Geikie, Phillips, Murchison, Smith** and **Lyell.**

THE JURASSIC DEPOSITS were laid down below the sea and include, depending on the depth of the water, sandstone, muds, silts, shales and limestones, many of these **rich in fossils.** Movements of the earth's crust over countless millennia caused erratic tilting which exposed different **mineral layers** along the coast. Some of these were more resistant than others to the constant battering of the waves, thus producing the **unique shape** of the North Yorkshire coastline.

PERHAPS THE MOST IMPORTANT ROCKS are those of the early **Lower Jurassic Period,** also referred to as **the 'Lias',** which means flat stone. The strata of the Lias are mainly comprised of shale with occasional bands of limestone and sandstone. The Lias have yielded much mineral wealth over the years, primarily **alum, ironstone** and **jet.**

Alum was important in **tanning,** the **dyeing** of cloth, and **calico printing.** During the C14th and C15th imports grew until the first discovery of alum in Britain at Belman Bank near Guisborough in 1595.

Following the death of Charles II, the **Royal Monopoly on alum** ended and quarries developed at Great Ayton, Guisborough and Osmotherley. Along the coast **whole sections of cliff were removed** over the years - such as at Boulby, Kettleness, Sandsend, Saltwick and Ravenscar. The alum shale was burnt between layers of brushwood or coal, often piled to a

height of over 15 metres. The shale was then soaked in pits and the liquid drained off, boiled and left to crystallise. It has been years since the extraction of alum was carried out.

Ironstone was once collected from workings on or near to the shore, at locations including **Port Mulgrave, Runswick Bay** and **Robin Hood's Bay.** Several prominent headlands along the coast, such as at Staithes and Robin Hood's Bay, are comprised of these more resistant ironstone rocks, whilst the bays between the headlands have been formed by the erosion of much softer rocks such as shale.

Another mineral that was mined along the coast, of great importance for a while, was **jet.** This shiny, black mineral was obtained by combing the beaches or by digging mines into the cliffs. The carving of this mineral into **jewellery** reached its peak in Whitby around 1870, when 1400 people were employed.

JET HAD BECOME POPULAR following its display in the **Great Exhibition** of 1851 and **Queen Victoria's** later adoption of it as mourning jewellery. But so sudden are changes in fashion that by 1885 only 300 people were still in employment. **Relics of the jet mines** can still be found today, and pieces of jet still lie on the beaches.

All this mineral extraction has revealed **a wealth of fossils,** including plentiful **ammonites, belemnites, marine reptiles** such as **plesiosaurs** and **ichthyosaurs** (some as much as 12 metres long), and the occasional **fish.** Fossils were formed in two main ways: either when impressions of shells or skeletons were left in the mud and silt of the Lias layers, or when mud filled the shells and formed moulds of their hollow interiors.

AN INTERESTING LOCAL LEGEND explains the **ammonites,** fossilised Mollusca shells, which are known locally as **'St Hilda's Snakes'.** Tradition tells how Hilda 'prayed the heads off' the snakes, which then curled up and turned to stone. In addition to shells and some bones, there are tremendous fossil remains of **plants** and even **dinosaur footprints!** Indeed, jet is itself of fossil origin, being formed from the wood of a **prehistoric tree** similar to today's monkey puzzle and which was common in this area.

Visitors should not attempt to remove fossils from the cliffs, which may be unstable - there are, in fact, plenty in the rock debris below. Good examples of all the main types can be seen at the **Whitby Museum, the Rotunda Museum** in Scarborough and **the Moors Centre** in Danby, all useful sources of information.

Landforms of the Moors

We have already looked at the **geological background** to the North York Moors and the processes which, over **millions of years,** have shaped this area. We have seen a general pattern emerge, explaining the form the landscape now takes and leaving us with that beautiful alternation of hills and dales that makes the North York Moors so appealing.

Here and there, that process has left **something special** behind: an outcrop of harder rock has withstood the force of the glacial meltwaters and the debris they carried; an area of softer rock has been more easily eaten into; **great forces underground** have produced sudden faults where the land is either split or up-tilted; **the action of the sea** has pulled away great chunks of coastline at some points and battered away to no effect at others; and finally **the wind and the rain** have also played their part in shaping our landscape. Between them, these forces have left us **many landforms** both beautiful and strange.

MOST BEAUTIFUL, PERHAPS, are the **waterfalls,** and many of them have suitably beautiful names: **Water Ark, Thomason** (or sometimes Thomasine) **Foss, Mallyan Spout** and **Falling Foss.** The first three of these are all quite close together near Goathland. Mallyan Spout, a sudden drop where the West Beck plunges down the Murk Esk Valley (one of Eskdale's loveliest tributaries) is **the highest** at 21 metres (70ft). It is best visited after rain. Otherwise, the amount of water falling in multiple rivulets down a mossy cliff may be rather sparse. Thomason Foss, on the other hand, is **a series of waterfalls** on the Eller Beck, and is much more generously fed. Indeed, it can be quite thunderous in wet weather conditions. At Falling Foss on the Little Beck, another tributary of the Esk Valley, the water rolls over **moss-covered rocks** before tumbling into a dark pool below.

Moving a few miles south, we find features of a different kind. **The Hole of Horcum** and **Blakey Topping** are related in legend if not in fact. The great Cleveland Giant, Wade, is said to have scooped up a handful of earth, leaving behind the Hole, and thrown it in a rage at his wife Bel, who ducked in time to let the clod of earth fall two miles beyond, forming Blakey Topping! In fact, **the huge natural amphitheatre** of the Hole of Horcum was created by water erosion, leaving a bowl of only partly fertile land. The **views** from its rim or from Saltergate Bank nearby are **exceptional.** Meanwhile, Blakey Topping is simply a harder than average outcrop of sandstone which has inevitably better withstood the forces of erosion and weathering to remain a prominent landmark.

A couple of miles to the south again, sandstone layers of differing durability have been worn by the action of the wind, rain and frost into the weird shapes known as **the Bridestones.** It used to be incorrectly believed that prehistoric man had erected these stones (the presence of so many dykes, barrows and cairns in the area makes the error understandable) and romantic legends grew up about their use. In fact, though natural, they are **strange and romantic** enough in their own right, and now form part of an interesting local nature reserve.

SPECTACULAR VIEWS may be had from many other high points on the Moors. **Danby Rigg,** for instance, is a natural landform rendered even more impressive and mysterious by the works of primitive man. Here there are multiple stone cairns and earthworks, as well as traces of a stone circle, and the views are unsurpassed. Two spots on the edges of the moors also command panoramic views. To the north, **Roseberry Topping** is a mighty hill whose south-western escarpment has been made more abrupt by centuries of quarrying. Two miles away, the craggy outcrops of **Highcliff Nab** keep it company. At the south-west corner of the area, **Sutton Bank** commands perhaps the most breathtaking views of all. In the foreground are the limestone ridge of **Roulston Scar** and **Hood Hill** (possibly a place of human sacrifice in pre-Roman times), while beyond lies the endless fertile expanse of the Vale of York. Just below Sutton Bank is the smallest natural lake in the country, **Lake Gormire.**

A description of the coastal scenery follows in a later chapter, so we have room here only to mention the most spectacular of its natural features, such as the massive **Boulby Cliff** near Staithes; the great Bay at **Runswick** and the headland at **Kettleness;** the cliffs at **Whitby;** the fine scoop of **Robin Hood's Bay** with the famous geological fault of **Ravenscar** at its southern extremity; and the massive headland dividing the two famous bays of **Scarborough.** All these are natural features created by the action of the sea, which still eats away this coastline at a rate of more than five centimetres per year!

Lastly, brief mention must be made of the famous **Kirkdale Cave;** a hyena den of the late glacial period which was later submerged for a time by rising meltwaters.

A Region of Forests

ONE OF THE HABITATS found in the area is that of the coniferous forest, but this has been created by man during this century! It was in 1919 that the **Forestry Commission** was established to build up Britain's timber resources - and the North York Moors was an obviously suitable location, with **Dalby Forest** one of the first areas to be planted. Now there are over 20,000 hectares of forest in the region.

It was man's activities through the centuries that had removed the natural forests and caused the exposed upland soils to become impoverished and acidified. In the Roman era the region was well-covered with trees, and the **great hunting forest of Pickering** was famous in **Norman** times. But trees had been prevented from regenerating on the North York Moors by repeated burning and grazing, and in many areas this is still the case. Controlled burning during the winter keeps the heather young, healthy and capable of supporting sheep and grouse. Land for afforestation therefore has to be fenced against stock and deep-ploughed to improve drainage which is essential for a healthy root-system, vigorous growth and stability. The acid conditions were most suitable for conifers and, since the **Scots Pine** is the only native conifer to produce good timber, other species had to be introduced from abroad. **Pines, spruces** and **larch** have proved best at producing a good crop on a 50 to 60 year rotation, but **broadleaved trees** still form part of the crop in more sheltered and fertile areas and are gradually being given increased prominence in re-plantings. The majority of broadleaves are planted as amenity trees whilst **birch, rowan, holly** and **oak** commonly establish themselves naturally among the planted crop.

IN THE EARLY LIFE OF A FOREST all the plantations are of a similar age and the young trees soon form a closed canopy that excludes light from the land surface. In the mature forest, plantations form a patchwork of different age groups. Each year some plantations are thinned, others clearfelled, and previous clearings replanted. This **diversity of crop** within the commercial forest supports a wide range of wildlife and is enriched by the construction of ponds and the **careful management** of a particularly vulnerable or sensitive habitat.

WATCHING WILDLIFE in the forest requires a little skill, some luck and a lot of patience - but the forest environment provides an ideal home for many animals such as the **roe deer,** once nearly extinct locally but now numbering over 3000 in the forests along the southern fringes of the North York Moors. To the west of the region the **fallow deer** is also found, though in smaller numbers. Another attractive animal that may once again be present is the **pine marten. Fox** and **badger** are common, and the bird list includes **jay, nightjar, siskin, crossbill, great spotted woodpecker** and the migratory **waxwing.** The chief birds of prey are the **sparrowhawk, kestrel** and **tawny owl. Grey squirrels** are present but are unwelcome because of the damage they do to the trees, particularly the broadleaved species, but **bats** are encouraged by the provision of bat-boxes.

THE FIRST FORESTS PLANTED in the area are now mature and are being felled, so the main work today is in re-planting, which amounts to some 240 hectares per year. The trees felled are mostly sold as sawlogs, with a small amount being pulped and some 10% sold for use as poles. But this is no ordinary commercial enterprise - why not come and see? **The Visitor Centre** in **Low Dalby Village** is open daily from April to October and contains a wealth of information on the locality. In addition there are picnic places, waymarked walks, **the Bridestones Nature Reserve** and forest wildlife. For the adventurous there is a wayfaring course and, for the less energetic, peace and quiet. **The Dalby Forest Drive** gives ready access along its nine-mile length to features such as Dalby Beck, Staindale Lake, the Adderstone and Crosscliffe Viewpoint.

A novel way to see part of **Cropton Forest** is to take a trip on the **North York Moors Historical Railway.** Running from Pickering to Grosmont (where it meets the Esk Valley Line) the passenger is treated to some of the best scenery in the North York Moors National Park. **Newtondale** was cut by a raging torrent of glacial meltwater which flowed south into the Vale of Pickering during the Ice Age. **Waymarked walks** leading from the Newtondale rail halt permit passengers to stretch their legs and take advantage of the splendid views from precipitous valley sides.

A stay at **Spiers House Camp Site** or in one of the forest cabins at **Keldy Cabins** is a marvellous opportunity to experience life in the forest. Situated in the heart of **Cropton Forest,** either centre makes an ideal base from which to explore the surrounding area of either the bleak and windswept moorland or the sheltered and secluded dales nestled among an expanse of heather. Furthermore, most of the villages and small market towns fringing the Vale of Pickering are of great antiquity.

Wildlife of the Moors & Dales

It is important for us to remember that the wildlife of the moors has not always been the same, with the major catalyst of change being the climate. During the **glacial periods,** part of the North York Moors was a nunatak above the surrounding sea of ice, an island of rock experiencing the **tundra conditions** of the present **Arctic.** In contrast, the inter-glacial periods brought climates that were much warmer than we experience today. Consequently the flora and fauna have been widely different and rapidly changing. The natural cover of the area was once **forests** of oak, birch, elm and hazel, as has been proved by a study of seeds and pollen found in the moorland peat deposits. **Man** has been largely responsible for the removal of all this natural tree cover, which has now been long gone - but the area is in no way less beautiful or 'natural' in appearance.

Today, it is the **heather-clad moorlands** that make the North York Moors so popular. From late August when the **scotch heather** or **'ling',** as it is known locally, is in full bloom, there is a purple blanket that stretches as far as the eye can see, covering the largest expanse of upland heath in England. By tradition it reaches its peak of perfection on the **18th of August,** but it lasts well into September. Two other heathers, the **cross-leaved heather** and **bell heather** add colour in July, whilst bilberry, bracken and rush add splashes of bright green which turn yellow and russet in autumn - the whole area is one of ever changing natural colours. Note that several rare species are to be found in the area, including bog rosemary and dwarf cornel, whilst in one of the northern valleys can be found **juniper,** one of Britain's true native conifers.

OF THE MOORLAND BIRDS, the **red grouse** is the most common with up to one dozen being born every spring in each nest - but soon subject to the hazards of the grouse shooting season which commences on the 'glorious' twelfth of August! Other moorland birds include the **curlew** which is most common during the nesting season, along with **lapwings** and **golden plover. Kestrels** and a small number of **merlins** are joined in winter by **snow-buntings** and an occasional **hen harrier. Skylarks, whinchats** and **wheatears** will be heard, if not seen.

ADDERS, WHICH ARE POISONOUS, are quite common, particularly in the rocky areas where they like to bask in the sun. They will not normally attack unless surprised or trapped but, although their bite is not normally fatal, hospital treatment should be sought immediately. They can be distinguished from the non-poisonous grass snake by **the V or X mark** behind their head. Another creature that is quite common is the **fox,** often seen crossing the moorland roads, usually at night. Indeed, in Dalby Forest, some rangers claim to have identified a sub-species of fox, longer-legged and grey in colour, but naturalists dispute this! One of the **insects** attracted to the moors in the summer is the **honey bee** which produces an excellent heather honey through to September. In the past, man would use straw as 'hives' but today rows of wooden hives are a very common sight. The **green hairstreak** and **common heath butterflies** are regularly found on the moors.

THE VALLEYS which dissect the moorland offer a very different landscape and environment. Here there are still some areas of dense, **broad-leaved woodland** containing **ash, sycamore, beech, oak** and **wild cherry.** Within these woodlands can be found a whole host of **other plants,** including **bluebell, St John's wort, wild angelica, wood anemone, dog's mercury, woodruff, forget-me-not, wood sorrel** and **lily of the valley** - to name but a few! **The insect, bird and animal life** is also rich and varied. Common birds include the **woodpecker, tree creeper, tawny owl,** several species of **tit** and **finch** and, close to streams, **wagtails, kingfishers, dippers** and **mallard duck. Badgers** also reside in these woodlands but, being nocturnal, are rarely seen during the day. **Fallow** and **roe deer** may be seen in many woodlands, as well as **squirrels, stoats, voles** and **mice.**

Even within the valleys, changes are evident. The more open and exposed valley sides, especially on the **limestone rocks** and soils to the south of the area, have a different variety of species. Commoner plants include **hairy violet, bloody cranesbill, rock rose** and **salad burnet,** while rarer plants such as **orchids** grow in several locations. In fact, on the flank of one valley (which must remain nameless) is the only place in the whole of Britain where the rare **may lily** grows wild. Finally, **wild daffodils,** once endangered, are now found in abundance in Farndale, where they have become a famous sight in spring.

Visitors should not pick rare plants nor handle a young bird or hare. Birds are happy to feed their fledglings on the ground at considerable distances from the nest, and mother hares deliberately distribute their leverets over a wide area for safety. The more we leave untouched, the more remains for other visitors to enjoy.

Wildlife of the Coast

Although the largest proportion of the area covered in this book is the North York Moors, we must also consider briefly the wildlife of the **long but narrow coastal strip** that comprises such an important element of this tremendous region.

In several places the moorlands actually merge with the cliffs that overlook **the North Sea.** In other places man has cultivated the land right up to the cliff edge and little space remains for coastal flora, let alone fauna.

THE EFFECT ON THE CLIFFS of the constant battering by the sea and the weather has been to create a mass of ledges, holes and caves, which provide **perfect nesting sites** for a great variety of seabirds. Some resourceful species make use of man-made sites as well, such as jetties and breakwaters.

THE COMMONEST BIRD is the ubiquitous **herring gull,** a scavenger and one of the least shy gulls, which is seen as frequently in the coastal villages as on the cliffs. The less bold **glaucous, lesser black-backed, common** and **black-headed gulls** are mainly seen in the winter months on the cliffs. The **great black-backed gull,** one of the most easily identified, is the least frequently seen. It is a fairly solitary bird, territorial in its habits and quite ready to attack other species.

While all these gulls may be seen in or near the coastal villages, the **kittiwakes,** though very numerous, are only found on the most inaccessible stretches of coast. These smaller, more streamlined birds, with their distinctive piping call and black wingtips, are most attractive.

Sharing the remoter cliff nesting sites are the **fulmars,** looking like gulls but actually relatives of the albatross. They have a habit of vomiting over intruders and are very accurate shots, so be warned!

IN THE SUMMER MONTHS many **terns,** distinguished by their forked 'swallow-tails', visit the coast and are to be seen diving for fish in the waters just offshore. A much less elegant fisherman is the large, black **cormorant,** either seen skimming across the waves or sitting on the rocks with wings apparently held out to dry.

In addition to the cliff-dwelling birds, there are many shore birds to be found wading among the rocks at low tide. The handsome **oystercatcher** and the less flashy **redshank** are among the larger ones, though you may be lucky enough to see a **curlew** too.

The charming **ringed plovers, turnstones** and **sandpipers** are found scurrying among the stones, and the tiny **rock pipit** may be seen flitting up the cliffs. And for the patient birdwatcher, there may be the thrill of seeing one of the rarer visitors to the coast, such as the **red-throated diver** or the **eider duck.**

THE ROCK POOLS ON THE SHORE are rich in marine species, with a wide range of **seaweeds, crabs, anemones, small fish** and many forms of **shell life.** The variety of colour can be spectacular, with red and green **anemones** endlessly opening and closing their tentacles in search of food, shiny black **sea urchins** and shells ranging from white **cockles** to blue-black **mussels. Translucent prawns and shrimps** dart about, and the **hermit crab,** with his borrowed winkle shell on his back, may scurry across the sandy floor of a pool. Larger **crabs** may suddenly be glimpsed lurking under a rock-shelf, when the green **seaweed** or rich brown **bladderwrack** is swept aside by a wave. Once captivated by this fascinating underwater world, you may find that you spend many happy hours discovering more, whilst enjoying the beauties and relaxing influence of the sea-shore.

FOR THE BOTANIST, the coast has much to offer, and a good place to visit is the **Wild Flower Reserve at Robin Hood's Bay,** where you may see such plants as **sea plantains, wild thyme, coltsfoot** and **giant horsetails** - all plants which are reasonably salt-tolerant. The horsetails have been here since prehistoric times, as the fossil record shows. Other, rarer finds may include **sea buckthorn, sea beet** and **sea rocket** but, even if you are no expert, the unexpected variety and quantity of plants clinging to these windswept cliffs will delight you.

The area as a whole has been popular with naturalists for many years. If you have an interest in natural history, then you should also enjoy a visit to the **Wood End Natural History Museum** in Scarborough or the **Pannett Park Museum** at Whitby.

Information on Nature Reserves may be obtained from the **Yorkshire Naturalists' Trust** at York. An earlier chapter deals with the nature of the Moors and Dales, covers the flora and fauna you may expect to find inland and details the interesting contrasts to be found within this splendid region as a whole.

Moors, Hills & Dales

For the purposes of this chapter, the 'Hills' are the **Cleveland, Hambleton** and **Tabular Hills**, and the 'Dales' are that lovely series of dales running side by side off these same hills, in a southerly direction, into the **Vale of Pickering.**

FROM WEST TO EAST, the chief ones are **Bilsdale** (itself a tributary of **Ryedale**), **Bransdale, Farndale** and **Rosedale.** Continuing to move east along the southern edge of the moors towards the coast, the same pattern is repeated but now the hills are flatter - which gives them their name, the **Tabular Hills** - and the dales are less frequent, the most important being **Newtondale** (down which the North York Moors Railway runs from Grosmont to Pickering), **Thornton Dale** and the **Forge Valley.** By this point, we are only a few miles inland from Scarborough. A later chapter deals with the valley of the River Esk, and the small, narrow dales which lead into it from the northern edge of the moors.

This alternating landscape of **heather-clad moorlands,** intersected by **green and fertile valleys,** is what gives the North York Moors their special appeal. If the moors share a certain impressive singleness of character, there are nevertheless dramatic vantage points to be found, which do something to relieve the vast expanses of wildness and desolation.

THE CLEVELAND HILLS, for instance, offer **Roseberry Topping** and **Hasty Bank,** both on the northern fringes, and the National Park's highest point at **Botton Head** on **Urra Moor** (454 metres/1,490ft). **The Hambletons'** most spectacular views are found at **Sutton Bank;** and even the heavily forested **Tabular Hills,** which appear to be chopped off along the long limestone escarpment, from **Rievaulx Moor** in the west to **Silpho Moor** in the east, offer some spectacular views.

But for real variety of character, it is to the dales that the visitor will turn. **Each dale has its own personality and charm,** and although there is not enough space here to detail them all individually, there is room to hint at the wide range of attractions they offer. One noticeable differentiating feature is the stone used both for buildings and dry-stone walls. The stone found in the lower dales to the south of the Park comes from **the limestone belt** which forms the Hambleton and Tabular Hills. This varies from

greyish-white to a more golden colour around Helmsley, where there are higher levels of sand and iron in the stone. Meanwhile, **in the upper dales the stone is chiefly sandstone,** giving the houses a much warmer, honey-coloured or even brown colouring. At one time almost every village in the limestone belt had its quarry, supplying both building stone and lime for fertiliser, while the richly-coloured sandstone was also very much in demand. Some was even used in building **the Houses of Parliament!**

CHARACTERISTICS which identify the valleys include, for instance, the famous **wild daffodils** which clothe the banks of the River Dove in spring, as it flows through Farndale; or the **exceptional beauties** of Rosedale, today so quiet and rural but once a hive of industry. Lonely, abandoned houses in upper Rosedale testify to this lead-mining period, and the **Ryedale Folk Museum** in **Hutton-le-Hole** reminds us of an earlier industry that thrived here in the time of Elizabeth I, glass-blowing.

NEWTONDALE, which runs south to Pickering, is of a different and altogether more dramatic character. It is hard to believe that this **impressive gorge,** cut by glacial meltwaters some 10,000 years ago, was probably created within two or three decades. Perhaps your best way of enjoying this dale is to take a ride on the **North York Moors Railway,** thereby sharing an experience with many earlier sightseers, among them **Charles Dickens!**

THORNTON DALE, fed by the Dalby Beck, is a pretty wooded dale which contains the excellent interpretive centre of the **Forestry Commission** at Low Dalby. From here one can follow the Dalby Forest Drive some ten miles along a toll-road that gives access to Dalby Beck, Staindale and several excellent viewpoints. Meanwhile, the **Bridestones Nature Reserve** is nearby, and the village of **Thornton-le-Dale** itself must rank as one of Yorkshire's most beautiful.

Finally we reach the **Forge Valley,** again much noted for its beauty and now a National Nature Reserve. The ancient village of **Hackness** is a favourite stopping place for visitors to this last dale before the coast.

What most needs to be added, perhaps, to the above brief descriptions, is some evocation of the **ever-changing moods** of this most appealing landscape. Bright green in spring, richly-coloured in summer, glowing purple and brown in autumn, the changes of mood are limitless. But remember too that, when few visitors are present, winter here is tough and the moors and dales return to their age-old loneliness.

Rural Farming Tradition

The North York Moors have been farmed for many hundreds of years. Indeed farming is the sustaining force in the area, and the shape of the landscape owes almost as much to the people who have farmed it as to nature herself. The **drystone walls,** for example, which sprawl so elegantly round the countryside, are the result of the backbreaking clearance of the fields by generations of unknown labourers.

THE WALLS, however, are the least of the changes in the landscape: the fields themselves owe their existence to **human endeavour.** Once, much of the area was forested with oak, birch, elm and hazel. These have been cleared over the centuries for the benefit of farmers, and many of the older dwellings in the area, as in the Market Place at Pickering, contain timber from the **ancient forests.** There are still some areas of dense, broad-leaved woodland containing ash, sycamore, beech, oak and wild cherry in the valleys which dissect the moorland.

A peaceful farming scene in Eskdale

THIS DIVISION BETWEEN VALLEY AND MOOR has had a significant effect on the area: the valleys belong to the **arable farmers,** who kept the watermills and windmills of Yorkshire busy for at least six centuries: Tocketts watermill, last survivor of the once prolific **working mills** of Cleveland, bears witness to this: its collection of millwright's tools and milling equipment shows that the water wheel has milled for over twenty-four generations of customers.

The hills and moorlands, however, have always been a much less forgiving environment for farmers, and yet it is this that has chiefly given the area its character: sheep. The moorlands, such as those above Pickering, belong to **sheep** and to grouse. Controlled burning of the heather on the moors during the winter keeps them a suitable habitat for the animals.

THE MONKS who once owned the abbeys of **Rievaulx** and **Byland** typify the balance of farming in the area in past times. They had vast interests in sheep farming and fisheries producing the income to keep them in the style from which **Henry VIII** eventually banished them at the **Dissolution of the Monasteries** in 1538.

Yorkshire was, in fact, once the centre of the world for **the wool trade.** Lealholm, an ancient village in the Esk Valley, even has a **Shepherds' Hall** with an engraved stone which portrays the **Ancient Order of Shepherds,** and the village green is kept in trim by sheep belonging to the local farmers who still have grazing rights throughout the village. **Sheep** are, in fact, so much a feature of the whole area, that in Goathland, the bus shelters have been fitted with gates to prevent sheep from using them in poor weather!

The whole of the North York Moors is criss-crossed by **drovers' roads**: in an age without motorised transport, the farmers would shoe all their livestock, even sheep, with metal to save their hooves on the long way to market.

If you want to experience the rural traditions of this area of Yorkshire, there is no better place to go than the award-winning **Ryedale Folk Museum,** in the attractive village of Hutton-le-Hole on the southern edge of the National Park. Opened in 1964, it is dedicated to preserving reminders of the daily lives of the people of Ryedale from prehistoric to recent times, and is a good record of the crafts and records which grow out of and support agriculture. Its most exciting exhibits are the old houses and cottages, rescued from dereliction elsewhere, and rebuilt at the museum.

A more modern record of farming tradition is **Thorpe Hall Farm,** near Ampleforth. With forty tractors, numerous hay-turners and balers, potato spinners and ploughs, and even a Dennis Fire Engine that children and adults alike will want to sit in, and a couple of donkeys joining the usual farmyard animals, it provides a memorable day out.

Cleveland's Coast & Countryside

The natural beauties of the Cleveland Coast and the Cleveland Hills, as well as a wealth of accommodation, entertainment and facilities, make this a region worthy of discovery and enjoyment in its own right, as well as a base from which to explore the North York Moors and Coast.

REDCAR The 'popular' resort of Cleveland, Redcar offers all the entertainment and relaxation a holidaymaker could wish for. Beautiful beaches and children's entertainments add up to a perfect holiday for all the family, and with miles of golden sands, you can easily find that secluded spot to relax, without having to worry about the safety of the children. Redcar's indoor fun fair, the largest of its kind in the North East, will attract both young and old alike, while the 'sport of kings' can be enjoyed at Redcar's racecourse, offering regular two and three day meetings during the May-October flat race season. The nightlife of Redcar is designed to suit all tastes and all age groups, with dancing, discotheques and nightclubs. Regular pop, folk and rock concerts are a feature of the Redcar Bowl's musical fare, where visitors are sure of a warm and friendly welcome. Summer attractions include the annual week-long carnival (late July) with entertainment for everyone. Brass band concerts, street entertainers, Punch and Judy, beach sports and games are all firm favourites throughout the season. The three main parks in Redcar, renowned for their floral beauty, offer the usual tennis courts, putting and bowling greens; and at **Locke Park,** amid tree-lined walks, are to be found lake fishing and boating, roses and rock gardens.

If you are historically minded, then the village of **Kirkleatham,** just two miles from the sea-front, is rich in buildings of architectural interest. Visit the 'Old Hall' museum, a restored Queen Anne building dating from 1710, with an aviary picnic site, large playground and nursery as well. **The Charles II Almshouses,** dating from 1662 and built in the style of Christopher Wren, are now the Sir William Turner Homes for the Elderly. **The Chapel** and the **Turner Mausoleum** can be visited on request.

SALTBURN Set high above the sea and shore, Saltburn has a unique and distinctive period charm. In contrast to Redcar, its qualities are of a quieter and more restful nature. Much of the **Victorian elegance** of this once spa town

remains, overlooking both sea-cliffs and woodland. In this sheltered wooded valley, the colourful **Italian Gardens** - almost as they were when designed in the 1860s - afford protection to tender plants and humans alike. Riftswood, a continuation of the valley, unspoilt and enchanting, offers peace and tranquillity. Of course, here too are the ingredients of every seaside holiday: a boating lake and funfair, flat sandy beaches and rock pools - a beachcomber's delight. For the energetic, here is the start of the long-distance walk, the **Cleveland Way,** either westwards over the moors or southwards up the towering Huntcliff and along the coast. For the less energetic, the restored C19th hydraulic **Cliff Tramway** saves the steep walk from beach to town. **Saltburn Pier** is the longest - and indeed the only - real pleasure pier on the North East coast.

Along the flat beach towards Redcar, the small quiet resort of **Marske** offers an ideal spot for a family picnic on the sands. Here too is the old churchyard of **St Germain's,** where **Captain Cook's father and sister** lie buried, and the distinctive Jacobean **Marske Hall,** now a Cheshire Home. Set in open country, just a short distance from the town, you will find **the tiny church at Upleatham** which at 17ft 9ins by 15ft is reputed to be the smallest in England.

GUISBOROUGH Situated slightly inland, this historic town, the ancient capital of Cleveland, can trace its history back before the **Domesday Book** to Saxon times. Outstanding among the many places of interest in this attractive market town are the remains of **the Priory,** first endowed in 1119, the medieval octagonal dovecot, market cross and Church of St Nicholas. Visit on a market day (Thursday or Saturday) when the colourful stalls line each side of the historic Westgate.

The North York Moors and the imposing Cleveland Hills are on the doorstep - why not visit the tiny village of **Newton** lying beneath the shelter of **Roseberry Topping?** It is worth climbing to 349 metres (1144ft) for the remarkable view. Like Guisborough, the pleasant village of **Skelton** lies on the very edge of the National Park and makes a fine centre for exploring the truly beautiful countryside which surrounds it. Further east, **Loftus** is comfortably placed where sea and moorland meet. The magnificent 201 metre high sea cliffs at **Rockcliffe,** the highest point on the East Coast of England, are within walking distance, giving breathtaking views. Huddling near their foot is the quaint fishing village of **Staithes** offering peace and solitude. Here is the northern gateway to the North York Moors National Park and its 553 square miles of unspoilt natural beauty.

The Esk Valley

AT ESKLETS, high and remote on **Westerdale Moor,** several streams converge to form the River Esk, which then meanders east, through **a pretty wooded valley** and alongside spreading villages and farmland, all the way to Whitby. Only occasionally, as at **Crunkley Ghyll** near Lealholm, does it thunder dramatically through a gorge. Otherwise, the Esk Valley offers a gentle, rural scene, perhaps best appreciated from the **Esk Valley Railway Line.**

It is well worth stopping, however, to enjoy the villages along the way. The first is **Castleton,** where only the earthworks of the Norman castle now remain. In the early days of the railway, Castleton flourished through its stone and silica quarries, but today it is quieter. The church has Robert Thompson (Mouseman of Kilburn) furnishings. In next door **Danby Dale** is **Botton,** where the famous Camphill Trust village for the mentally handicapped welcomes visitors. Nearby, **Danby Beacon** offers fine views from a height of 299 metres (980ft).

Danby itself offers much of interest. The semi-ruined walls of **Danby Castle,** built in the C14th by the Latimer family, dominate the village. Here **Catherine Parr,** then wife of the third Lord Neville, was wooed by **Henry VIII,** finally becoming his sixth wife. Danby's **Duck Bridge** is another medieval survival; and thought to be even older in origin is the local sport of **quoits** (possibly learnt from the Romans) and hotly contested at the annual 'Danby Open'. Don't miss the National Park's Moors Centre at Danby.

Another appealing stopping place is the ancient riverside village of **Lealholm,** also a centre for quoits. This village has much of interest: the village stepping stones, the Shepherds' Hall, the Quaker Burial Ground, and the 'Hart Stones' on Lealholm Rigg, left by two huntsmen to mark the spot where a deer they were chasing made a massive 12 metre (40ft) leap! Note the name 'Park' in many house names; this was a baronial hunting park.

The next stretch of the valley from Lealholm to **Egton** is probably the most beautiful, despite its past links with iron ore mining. Much older are the stone causeways seen here, for this was a major trading route in the days of drovers and pannier ponies. Don't miss the beautiful, single-arched **Beggar's Bridge** of 1619, reputedly built by Thomas Ferris of Glaisdale, who had to ford the river Esk to visit his sweetheart in Egton. Once he had made his fortune abroad, he paid for the bridge to be built so that future young lovers could meet in a drier condition! Egton is a windswept, hill-top village, well known for its annual **Gooseberry Show,** held in August.

The next stop is **Grosmont,** a 'modern' C19th iron-ore mining village. Near the present Grosmont Farm there was once a priory, founded around 1200 and dissolved in 1539, one of only three established by the **Grandimontine Order** in England. The Esk Valley Line links with the North Yorkshire Moors Railway at Grosmont, and the nearby villages of **Beck Hole** and **Goathland** (not strictly in the Esk Valley) deserve mention. You can reach these settlements via the Historical Railway Trail. Beck Hole, despite its mining origins, is a beautiful place, a tiny hamlet famous for its inn sign by Algernon Newton, R.A. - and for its tradition of playing quoits.

Goathland is a much more ancient settlement whose name, formerly 'Godeland', may be of **Norse origin** or may indicate a place of religious importance. It is loosely spread around a huge green, like Lealholm's kept in trim by local sheep. And again, old paved causeways or 'trods' indicate that this was, improbably as it now seems, a major routeway between Whitby and Pickering. The church contains an early C15th chalice, one of only two of its kind known. Nearby is the village pinfold, where stray livestock were impounded until their owners redeemed them with a fine. It was last used in 1924, and 11 years later the chestnut tree at its centre was planted to celebrate the Silver Jubilee of King George

Returning to the Esk Valley proper, we approach **Sleights,** passing disused alum workings and the ruins of **Eskdaleside Chapel,** where, in 1159, a dying monk told huntsmen who had attacked him to plant a **'Penny Hedge'** as a penance. The Abbot of Whitby ruled that a hedge should indeed be planted in the mud of Whitby harbour, using only penny knives, and the penance has been carried out on Ascension eve ever since. Passing through the famous stone-quarrying village of **Aislaby,** and the ancient settlement of **Briggswath** ('wath' is Norse for ford), which has so often been disastrously flooded, we come to **Ruswarp,** a delightful holiday centre with its old mill, pub, weekly auction mart, and even 9-hole hillside golf course! The Esk River is perhaps most beautiful at this point, adorned with a rich variety of bird life and excellent fishing (day tickets are available) Finally, we reach the charming seaside town of **Whitby,** which is more fully described in its own chapter.

'Heartbeat Country'

As we pass through the landscape of the North York Moors and Coast, we can gain no more than a superficial sense of its personal character and the beat of its living heart. Even if we could walk throughout the district, and visit every place in this guide, it is possible that we would still feel no more than visitors. But thanks to **Yorkshire Television's 'Heartbeat'** (Heartbeat is a trademark of Yorkshire Television Limited), the life of the landscape is captured for us on screen, so that we can deepen our understanding and enjoy it all the more.

To further enhance your enjoyment of this remarkable region, we have published our **'Heartbeat Country'** guidebook in our Heritage Series of full colour publications. It provides an informative and photographic representation of this area that so many of us have come to love and cherish.

An interesting scene at Grosmont Station

'Heartbeat Country' is situated in the heartland of the North York Moors National Park extending approximately twenty miles around the village of **Goathland,** and is comprised of both coastline and countryside.

Goathland is known as Aidensfield in the 'Heartbeat' television series, and much of the location filming for the programme is done there. However, many of the other locations are a closely guarded secret as everyone is well aware of the distractions and inconvenience it may cause to local residents and their way of life when a television series becomes very popular.

It is certainly pleasing that people who may never have had the opportunity to experience the splendour of the North York Moors can now savour it on their television screens. Heartbeat is about coming to terms with the environment as well as actual police work and relationships between people. In this respect the great audience it attracts can relate in more than a superficial way to the pace of living in this glorious area, with the added attraction of the great outdoors.

The North York Moors and Coast is not only special and interesting; above all it is inspiring. It is an area that has been described by some writers as resembling both the beautiful Cotswolds in the sandstone countryside of its northern valleys and like the West Country in its magnificent coastline: two beautiful landscapes of natural and national importance rolled into one happy coincidence.

It has been said that **Nicholas Rhea,** the author of the **'Constable' books** on which the Heartbeat series is based, is to the country policemen of North Yorkshire what **James Herriot** is to the vets. Like Herriot, Nicholas Rhea (a pen-name for ex-Police Inspector Peter N. Walker) wrote the books from experience, some thirty years in the police force of the North Riding of Yorkshire. His love of the landscape of the North York Moors has, also like Herriot's, a bittersweet comic touch which takes you to the heart of a character more quickly than many a 'serious' book might. Then, through the powerful medium of television, this special landscape has been popularised with millions of viewers.

Now visitors arrive to ride on the **North Yorkshire Moors Railway** which features so largely throughout the Heartbeat series; or visit the station at Pickering, scene of so many tearful goodbyes as Aidenfield's station; or walk across Goathland's village green where the police house is located; or have a drink in the Aidensfield Arms; or visit the country church nestling peacefully in a canopy of trees under the rolling hills of Allen Tofts.

It might seem strange that one of the industries most closely associated with the North York Moors is television, but we must remember that this area depends to a great extent on tourism to sustain its economy. And what is television, if not a chairbound type of tourism, a method of escape that allows you to sit still after a hard day's work? The North York Moors may yet live to thank Nick and Kate Rowan, Sergeant Blakeston, Claude Jeremiah Greengrass, and friends. Who knows: they might even pass into local legend, the real heartbeat of any area!

Thirsk, Helmsley, Pickering

No trip through the area would be complete without a wander round one of its market-towns, the ancient nerve centres of commerce, farming, and life. Even today, they retain the architecture and rural flavour of a century ago.

THIRSK This quaint market town, now mercifully by-passed by the A19, has regained its composure and has much to offer the visitor, despite the fact that only a few very old buildings remain. One of these is the impressive church of St Mary. Begun in 1430 and completed in the C16th, this sombre building with its buttressed tower and unexpectedly ornate parapet is probably the best example of perpendicular architecture in Yorkshire. Only faint traces of Thirsk Castle are seen, and the majority of buildings date from the C18th and C19th. Famous people associated with the town include **Thomas Lord,** the founder of Lord's Cricket Ground; **James Herriot,** the famous vet and author who worked in Thirsk; and **Bill Foggitt,** the well-known local weather forecaster who based his forecasts on annual changes in the weather.

HELMSLEY This wholly delightful historic market town is recorded as 'Elmslac' in the Domesday Book. The major historic building is undoubtedly the impressive **Helmsley Castle,** which influenced the growth and development of the town from the time of its construction in the C12th. Even today, in its ruinous condition, it dominates and overshadows the town.

Of the other historic buildings, the church is perhaps next in significance. Adjacent to the Market Place, it is Norman, though much renovated in the C13th and C15th. The wall mural, designed by the Reverend Mr Grey, who was vicar here from 1870 to 1913, is of interest. He was known as a great social reformer and builder, though the most ambitious of his schemes was never fulfilled. This was to rebuild **Rievaulx Abbey,** but he could not raise the (at the time) prodigious sum of £30,000 required for the job.

He was, however, successful in establishing the annual open air service, still held in the ruins of the Abbey. The vicarage he built in Bondgate, just off the Market Square, in 1900, is now the headquarters of the North York Moors National Park. **The Market Square** as a whole is notable for fine buildings and characterful coaching inns. Helmsley also contains interesting shops, and is an excellent base for touring the Dales.

Helmsley is ever popular with visitors

PICKERING This market town developed at the convergence of two major ancient routeways that retain their importance today as the A170 from Scarborough to Helmsley, and the A169 from Malton to Whitby.

It is a very old settlement, said to have been given the name 'Pickering' in 270BC by **King Peredurus.** He is reputed to have lost a ring in a local stream and later to have recovered it from the belly of a pike that he ate. However, the town only began to grow in importance with the coming of the Normans, and the building of **Pickering Castle,** a royal hunting lodge, in the C11th. It is still standing.

Perhaps the oldest part of the town is the sloping Market Place, once the village green. The shop fronts are modern, but the buildings are evidently of great antiquity. Many still incorporate oak cut in medieval times from the **Royal Forest of Pickering,** part of which, to the north of the town, is still in the ownership of the monarch.

The church of St Peter and St Paul, at the top of the market place, is C12th, and is known for the excellence of its C15th murals, discovered in 1853 under layers of whitewash. They depict various biblical scenes, along with **St George** slaying the dragon, and the murder of **Thomas à Becket.**

Not far away, near the town centre, is Pickering station, the southern terminus of the famous **North Yorkshire Moors Railway.** The station also has a bookshop and information centre.

Heritage Coast

We have already described the Cleveland Coast which stretches from Redcar to Boulby Cliff. To the south of this, a long stretch of the coast described in our guide (from **Boulby** nearly to **Scarborough**), falls within the North York Moors National Park. Boulby is an appropriate point at which to separate the two, being the highest point, at 209 metres (690 ft). This southern stretch, plus the few extra miles down to Scarborough's boundary, has been identified as a **Heritage Coast** worthy of special protection. A further length of coast, south of **Filey** to **Flamborough Head** (which is itself now protected), has been proposed as a Heritage Coast; and the well-known, long distance footpath, **the Cleveland Way**, follows our coast from Saltburn to Filey. The 35 miles (57 km) of Heritage Coast from **Saltburn** to **Scarborough** are subject to greater recreational pressure than any other part of the North York Moors National Park. Special provision will therefore have to be made if this area, and indeed the rest of our coastline, is to remain beautiful, interesting and yet part of a living community. While nature undoubtedly controls our coastline to a very large extent, man has, over the centuries, made a permanent and often pleasant contribution, particularly in coastal settlements such as **Staithes** and **Robin Hood's Bay**.

Our brief survey extends from Staithes to Scarborough and includes the most dramatic and picturesque sections of this ancient coastline. The coast is dominated by rugged cliffs cut by occasional valleys that sweep down to the shore. **Boulby Cliff,** near Staithes, and **Speeton Cliffs,** near Flamborough, have little besides their height in common. Boulby Cliff, formed from dark grey shale, still shows the scars of C17th and C18th quarrying operations, while Speeton Cliffs, composed of brilliant white chalk, provide the nesting sites for thousands of seabirds. Beyond Staithes, the cliffs continue past **Port Mulgrave** (a grand title for so small a place), which grew up during the iron-mining boom of the C19th when ore from the Grinkle mines was moved the two miles to the port by narrow-gauge railway via three tunnels. Today the terraced miners' houses remain, though the harbour is decaying. There are fine views both here and at **Runswick Bay,** the first real bay on our length of coastline. This attractive little village, with its houses dispersed over the hillside, was, like Staithes, originally developed as a fishing community, but today draws a large

proportion of its income from the tourist trade. Runswick has proud memories, such as 1901 when, during a storm, the fishwives launched the lifeboat themselves to save their husbands. In the spring storms of 1682, virtually the whole village sank towards the sea, but all the residents escaped. The bay is well known to fossil hunters and artists.

Sandsend, as the name suggests, is where the sand finishes when travelling up the coast from Whitby. For us, therefore, it is where the sand begins, continuing for over 2½ miles. **Whitby** itself is unique. Its situation, facing due north on the east coast, backed by the high moorlands of north-east Yorkshire and dissected by the River Esk, has had a tremendous effect on the development and history of the town. The remains of the great Abbey on the east cliff overlook a town which, in many ways, has not changed for centuries. Evidence of its early jet, whaling and fishing industries can still be seen - along with reminders of some of its famous people: **Captain Cook, Captain William Scoresby, George Stephenson** and **Frank Meadow Sutcliffe.** For those interested in our past heritage, Whitby is an essential port of call. The clifftop walk from the Abbey to **Saltwick Nab** is probably the most heavily used section of cliff path on this coastline.

From the old alum works of **Saltwick,** we can continue south-east to **Robin Hood's Bay,** yet another gem on the Yorkshire Coast. This village, typical of most along the coast, is crowded onto the banks of a ravine which gives access to the shore. The bay itself is, after Filey Bay, the largest on the Yorkshire Coast. Carved into some of the oldest rocks in our area, it sweeps round in a huge crescent from **North Cheek** to **Ravenscar** in the south. Apart from the village, the bay is well known for its rich marine life, one reason why a marine laboratory has been established here. The imposing headland of Ravenscar is capped with a fine building whose castellated walls can be seen over three miles away at **Bay Town**. Once again the tremendous cliffs decrease in height as we move south, passing a number of 'wykes' - small indentations along the coastline. **Hayburn Wyke** and **Cloughton Wyke** are two of the best known of these small bays. Crossing **Scalby Beck,** we come to the outskirts of the popular holiday resort of **Scarborough** with its prominent headlands and sweeping bays.

The people of the coast have long traditions associated with the sea, including exploration and **navigation, whaling, fishing, smuggling** and, in more recent times, the trades and crafts connected with tourism. Here, then, is a mere cameo of the Yorkshire Coast; a library could not contain all there is to know.

Maritime Fishing Tradition

Fishing has always been the mainstay of the coastal settlements and, in fact, is the very reason for their existence. From the earliest times, the sea was a bountiful provider, a source of high protein food in the days before the arrival of the monastic foundations with their efficient farming methods. Today, there is a visible link with those early fishermen - the boats. Called **cobles,** and locally pronounced 'cobbles', they have barely changed in 1000 years. A coble is a small, flat-bottomed craft designed to carry three men, clinker-built (that is, with overlapping planks) and without a keel. They have a stylistic feature which is inherited from the great **Viking longships** in which the Norse invaders came: an unusually high bow. Their remarkable stability in high seas means they can be used all the year round.

By the late C18th and early C19th, fishing had developed into an industry, in which the small ports on our coastline were heavily engaged. **Whitby,** which may appear today to be the most substantial, was in fact outstripped in numbers of fishing boats by both **Robin Hood's Bay** and **Staithes.** White fish, such as cod, ling and turbot, were caught in the spring and early summer months, followed by herring. The fish would be auctioned at the quayside, before being transported by packhorse to the wealthy areas of west and south Yorkshire, or kept for 'curing', which meant being salted and dried, or smoked. The largely Catholic populations of the Mediterranean countries were major consumers of cured fish. With the advent of the railways in the 1880s, **fresh fish** could be sent as far afield as the Midlands and London. At this time, the wage for a hired hand was as much as 20 shillings a week - good money for the period.

Virtually the whole community was involved in some way - children making **lobster pots** and collecting mussels for bait; women making and repairing nets, baiting lines, gutting, cleaning and curing fish; and everyone helping launch boats or haul them ashore. And while the men were out, many wives would be knitting socks, hats and the well-known blue guernsey jumpers, here called **'ganseys',** the designs differing from village to village.

Everywhere, alongside the legitimate fishing industry, **smuggling** flourished well into the C19th. The many small coastal inlets and caves made ideal hiding places for such illicit goods as liquor or taxable luxuries like bales of silk. Smuggling was punishable by hanging, yet many local landowners still ran highly organised and profitable operations.

Another periodic source of income for the local people would be the salvage of items from **shipwrecks** which, having run aground, would be forced to offload their cargoes in an attempt to re-float. Heavily laden collier vessels were frequent victims - a beachcomber could earn a penny for a recovered pit-prop and as much as ninepence for a copper rivet.

The skilful and hardy local men were sought-after recruits for the **Merchant Navy.** For instance, in the mid C18th, over a quarter of the entire population of Robin Hood's Bay, men and boys alike, had joined, many unwilling and bullied into it by the feared **Press Gangs.** Whitby was by now a major merchant port, with about 400 vessels, many transporting alum and ironstone ore, which were mined locally. It was also **a whaling port,** with two vessels in 1753 having increased to 15 by 1776. At the peak, in 1814, eight whalers caught 172 whales, producing 1390 tonnes of oil and 42 tonnes of whale fins. Yet, by 1837, there were only two vessels - one unsuccessful, the other wrecked! The same fate lay in store for all these communities. **Steam trawlers,** able to fish for days on end, taking huge catches with factory nets, deprived local people of their livelihood. The local bays were too shallow and awkward of access to admit these larger boats and by the 1920s almost no-one was fishing in Runswick or Robin Hood's Bay, and even in Staithes only a handful of cobles were still operating. Whitby, with its **shipbuilding, sail** and **rope making** industries, fared only slightly better, and eventually there was little for any fisherman to do but take out a few tourists on a still day to admire the craggy coastline.

Today, there has been a slight revival. A few boats will be found in each of these ports, catching **lobsters** as they have for generations, but very little white fish. The trawlers had effectively fished out the **herring** until, rather late in the day, recent restrictions were brought in to try and save the situation. This move may have been made in time and the herring shoals do seem to be on the increase, though there is new concern about **mackerel.** Surprisingly, one of the most sought-after catches is now **salmon.**

You will still find many local people who have a wealth of stories and information built up over **generations of seafaring.** Though the fishing may not be what it was in its heyday, it is still in their blood, and proximity to the sea, with all its waywardness and danger, remains the major influence in their lives.

Staithes

THIS CHARMING COASTAL VILLAGE is full of character, huddling down to the harbour in low ranks of houses, as if crouching together will help them to survive the might of the sea. Here in 'Steers', as it is locally known, a tight-knit fishing community still lives, fiercely preserving a traditional and very ancient way of life. It has been fortunate to have seen a considerable **revival of the fishing industry** in recent years, unlike so many fishing communities on this coast. Staithes is now the tenth largest lobster port in England and Wales, though it also draws a proportion of its income from the tourist trade.

The first record of Staithes is in the **Domesday Book** of 1086. However, it is thought that the settlement is much older, although it would have been situated further inland as protection against the **Danish and Viking raids** which harried this coast in the Dark Ages. As the centuries passed, these raids gradually came to an end, and the settlement grew towards the sea and the landing-place that were to give it both livelihood and identity.

This gem among Yorkshire fishing villages was always very remote, more easily accessible by sea than by land, and consequently retained a distinctive character, developing **peculiar customs,** and a language almost of its own. Some local women still wear, on special occasions, the frilled and starched bonnets that are peculiar to this village, and many retain the skill of knitting, to very localised patterns, the **fishermen's 'ganseys'** or pullovers.

Like Robin Hood's Bay, Staithes was a great centre for **smuggling,** and has tales of the infamous 'Preventative Service', and of their search for smugglers. There are also stories of disaster at sea and the **heroism of the local lifeboatmen.** As much as the sea was a provider of food and income, it could be suddenly cruel and destructive. In 1815, 29 fishermen of Staithes and Runswick were lost in a storm. In the winter of 1988, the lifeboat itself was overturned by a mountainous wave. Fortunately the boat righted itself, and all but one of the crew returned safely home.

THE NORTH SEA CAN PUNISH THE HOUSES that lie beside it as well as to the people who lived in them and worked on the ships. The young **James Cook** served as an apprentice in Mr Sanderson's general dealer's shop but it, like so many houses in this quaint, cliff-clinging village, has long since disappeared, either washed into the sea by a storm in 1740, or in February 1831, or dismantled for fear of possible damage in 1812. No-one knows for sure, and the sea keeps its secrets.

The cottage today known as **Cook's Cottage,** which bears a plaque commemorating the inauguration of the **Heritage Trail** by the **Prince of Wales** in 1978, is said to incorporate material salvaged from the original house where Cook lived, according to legend, in an attic with other apprentices and sailors, while in Staithes. Cook might also recognise the 'Cod and Lobster' public house which stood beside Sanderson's shop, and is still here today, though much rebuilt.

The quaintness of Staithes and Cowbar

Despite the rigorous conditions on this coast, the village has fired the imagination of many visitors, as it did with Cook before them. Cook left Staithes for Whitby to seek a career on the sea, but others have stayed, among them the artist **Dame Laura Knight,** who lived and painted here for 18 years.

Staithes and the adjacent hamlet of **Cowbar** have a **fairy-tale setting** on a spectacular coastline, where the nearby Boulby cliffs at over 200 metres are among the loftiest precipices in England, and make magnificent walking. Climbing among the narrow, cobbled streets with their jumbled cottages; listening in the pubs to **old tales of smuggling and Press Gangs;** or watching the small cobles and trawlers in the harbour, today's visitor can share - yes, even in the twentieth century - a vision of a different era, a harsher past..

Whitby

THE QUAINT CHARACTER OF THE TOWN is a result of its long **maritime tradition,** the residents building their homes as close to the harbour as possible. Covering the steep valley sides on both banks of the River Esk, at its mouth the narrow streets, compact houses and red rooftops nestling below the lofty ruins of **Whitby Abbey** create an almost fairy-tale scene for the visitor. Perhaps the special appeal of Whitby results from its long and rich history. Flints have been found in the area dating from the **Stone Age.**

Whitby piers and harbour

THE FIRST AUTHENTIC RECORD of the existence of the town is found in the writings of the **Venerable Bede** in Saxon times. We learn of the foundation of the Abbey in AD 657 by **St Hilda;** of its role in the great religious debate over the dating of Easter at the **Synod of Whitby** in AD 664; and of its connection with **Caedmon,** the first writer of religious verse in English.

Caedmon was a shy cowherd who would retire to bed rather than join in the regular singing at the Abbey. On one such occasion he had a vision and upon waking sang the '**Song of Creation**' to Hilda. She immediately instructed that he should be taught the scriptures, so that he could sing these in verse as well. A memorial to Caedmon was unveiled in 1898 at the top of the church steps. On one side of this cross are the lines of his 'Song of Creation'. The graves of St Hilda and her successor Aelfled are to be seen in the adjacent Abbey.

AS THE ABBEY GREW IN IMPORTANCE,

so did the town. Indeed, mentioned in the Domesday Book of 1086, it was made a **free borough** before 1189 ... this only to be later repealed by **King John** after pressure from the Abbey who felt they were losing some of their power! The antiquity of the settlement can be seen in the street-names, such as Flowergate (1224), Haggersgate (1296), Kirkgate or Church Street (1318) and Baxtergate (1574). However, the streets then were probably little more than unpaved tracks lined with occasional small thatched cottages.

Whitby has always had its 'eyes to the sea', not only because of its resources but also because the moorland barrier surrounding the town prevented easy communication from inland. Two lighthouses with fixed beacons, one red and one green, now overlook the harbour entrance. The green one, to the west, is sometimes open to the public in the summer.

SHIPBUILDING, FISHING AND WHALING flourished, as did trade in the C17th and early C18th. Cargoes included foodstuffs such as butter, hams, bacon and salt fish. By the early C19th, Whitby was the **sixth largest port** in England, but later lost its eminent position as vessels became larger and harbour and port facilities became inadequate due to the limited depth of water.

THE WHITBY PIERS date from the time of Henry VIII, who owned much of the town and ordered their maintenance at royal expense. In 1632, they were reconstructed in stone, but their maintenance was always a problem. In 1906 the responsibility for the harbour and piers was taken over by the town, who commenced the construction of a 150 metre (500 ft) extension to each pier in 1907. This huge task was completed in 1914 and escaped destruction, although the abbey was damaged, when the town was **fired upon by two German cruisers** on December 16th 1914. An unusual and very interesting feature of the piers is that they **line up with the North Pole.** This is because the town, although on the east coast, faces north. Consequently it is possible in mid-summer, to stand on the cliffs and see the sun rise from, and set into, the sea.

FISHING has always been an occupation here, though **whaling** which once was so important is now only a part of the town's history. The most highly regarded of the whaling captains was **William Scoresby,** who for many years held the distinction of having penetrated further north into the perilous Arctic seas than any other navigator. He died in 1829 and is commemorated by a **whalebone arch** near the **Captain Cook monument.** The story of **Whitby's fishing community** is discussed fully in the chapter 'Maritime Fishing Tradition' and is traced at the **museum in Pannett Park.** As often with coastal towns, there are many tales of heroism associated with the **lifeboat.** Extreme danger, and sometimes self-sacrifice are the price the brave crewmen of the lifeboat pay for their courage. On February 8th 1861, twelve seamen were lost after rescuing several stricken crews.

The two other major industries of the town were the **extraction of alum** and **carving of jet,** an industry which in the early C19th employed 1500 men. This was at the peak of the town's importance as a seaport, but the writing was on the wall for the shipping industry, and the town knew it had to improve links with the inland population if its economy was to survive. A road system over the moors was not considered a viable option. **A plan for a canal** through the gorge of Newtondale to the Vale of Pickering had already been proposed, but abandoned because of the prohibitive cost.

THE C19TH BIRTH OF THE RAILWAYS brought new hope. It was originally suggested that a line should be linked to the **Stockton and Darlington Railway,** but **George Stephenson's advice,** in 1832, was to build it between Whitby and Pickering. Supervised by Stephenson, the horse-drawn line was completed and opened in May 1836. The following year the railway was converted to steam power, thanks to the financial backing of **George Hudson,** to whom the development of the town as a tourist resort can be attributed. In the C19th Whitby prospered as a **health resort,** offering **spa waters** and sea bathing, and today tourism is still an essential part of the economy of this appealing and distinctive town.

WHITBY IS A PICTURESQUE TOWN which breathes history, heritage and tradition. Its location on either side of the River Esk has meant that bridging the river has always been vital. A bridge has existed on the site of the present structure for some 600 years. One problem has always been access for vessels up-river, but this was overcome by a drawbridge built in 1766 and later by **swing bridges** in 1835 and 1909.

Among Whitby's major attractions are **the famous 199 steps** accompanied by the adjacent narrow, cobbled 'donkey road' leading to the eastern cliff top and **St Mary's Church.** Built by Abbot William de Percy circa 1110, possibly on the site of a Saxon Church, St Mary's is of unusual design, with its C17th roof having been made by ships' carpenters in their own style. In the churchyard, **Dracula** is reputed to be buried! For Whitby's connection with the story of Dracula, by **Abraham (Bram) Stoker,**

Castlegate Exhibitions of York have mounted a **'Dracula Experience'** in Whitby. Nearby are the ruins of **Whitby Abbey,** the town's major landmark, and the ancient **Abbey Cross.**

On the opposite bank of the river, the climb to the cliff tops is through the **'Khyber Pass',** hewn out of solid rock. Here you will find the **whalebone arch** and plaque commemorating **Captain William Scoresby** and the **Whitby whaling industry.** Nearby is the statue of **Captain James Cook** whose employer's home can still be seen in Grape Lane, housing the **Captain Cook Memorial Museum.** The ships which Cook commanded on his journeys around the world were built in Whitby.

In the C19th another famous Whitby resident was the photographer **Frank Meadow Sutcliffe,** who made a unique record of life in Victorian Whitby and whose work can be seen at the **Sutcliffe Gallery.**

Fishing boats in Whitby Harbour

Today, **Whitby prospers** partly from the tourist industry, a development helped by the now good rail and road links which make it accessible from other parts of the country. Its attractions include its **quaint appearance,** rich history, interesting museums, sandy beaches, cliff coastline and nearby moorlands of the North York Moors National Park. A centre to visit in its own right, Whitby also provides **an excellent base for the exploration** of the surrounding coast and countryside.

Robin Hood's Bay

To the south of Whitby, visitors will find the **charming coastal village** of Robin Hood's Bay: like Whitby itself, for many centuries more accessible by sea than by land. There is a fine 3 mile sandy beach, relatively sheltered by **North Point** or **North Cheek,** but the village itself is huddled on the cliffs, houses closely built along narrow lanes and fishing boats tied up below. Past erosion by the sea, estimated at six metres per century, is held back today by an extensive - and expensive - new sea wall.

The narrow winding streets of Robin Hood's Bay

THE BAY AND ITS VILLAGE were known as Robin Hood's Bay from at least as early as 1538. Legend has it that **Robin Hood,** otherwise known as Robert, Earl of Huntingdon, shot an arrow from his bow, saying that where it landed he would build a home. It landed on these cliffs. However, another story tells of how the outlaw, dressed in Lincoln Green, was chased here, and escaped by disguising himself as a local fisherman.

Fishermen here have needed to be a hardy breed for generations fishing from small cobles, braving wind and weather in all but the worst days of winter. Eventually the cobles were largely superseded by trawlers and even whalers, but the very increase in the size of the vessels spelt the end of fishing prosperity, as Robin Hood's Bay was too shallow and small to allow the bigger vessels in. However, a partial revival is under way with **lobster** and **salmon** fishing.

It was the **development of the railways** in the late C19th that saved Robin Hood's Bay from terminal decline, for the village is close enough to Whitby to have shared a certain amount of that port's increased prosperity - as witnessed by the building of the **Mount Pleasant** area, where the neat Victorian streets contrast with the jumble of ancient cottages below

THERE ARE MANY TALES in this area about the heyday of seafaring, with splendid stories of **smugglers** using the honeycombed cliffs for concealing their contraband goods, which ranged from tobacco and spirits to such luxuries as silk. As the **Exhibition Centre** in Chapel Street tells, Robin Hood's Bay was said to be the greatest centre for smuggling in the entire realm. Several houses still have secret rooms where smugglers could be concealed from the 'Preventative Service', always trying to apprehend them. The smugglers' hiding places were no doubt also useful for avoiding the notorious **Press Gangs,** who forcibly 'volunteered' men for the Royal Navy. In theory, fishermen were exempt, but their reputation as skilled seamen made them a regular target. Robin Hood's Bay has a street named **the Bolts,** down which such men are said to have escaped

Looking seaward over Robin Hood's Bay

ALL FISHING VILLAGES HAVE THEIR TALES OF HEROISM, none more so than Robin Hood's Bay. An inscription in the church tells of the Bay's first lifeboat, but even before there was a lifeboat at the Bay, there were **wrecks** at this point: a wreck occurred in 1881, in a storm so severe that the **Whitby lifeboat** could not be launched to help the stricken crew. **Undaunted,** the men of Robin Hood's Bay walked to Whitby, collected the lifeboat, carried it back over the moors and hills, and lowered it down the cliff face to save six lives.

Scarborough

Scarborough is one of the most beautiful, historic and popular resorts in England. Beside a mighty headland with C12th castle, it faces the North Sea across two wide sweeping sandy bays. The heart of the old town, with its red pantile roofs, narrow streets and long flights of steps leading down to the fishing vessels below, is found on the headland slopes above the harbour. From here, south along the foreshore of South Bay, there is a little 'Golden Mile' of amusements, shops and cafes. North Bay presents a very different picture, for here fine Regency terraces and hotels overlook the bay from the cliff tops.

THIS HOLIDAY RESORT has a wide variety of entertainment and leisure. The Scarborough Fayre is held in June; throughout the season there are events at the Spa Concert Hall, Theatre and Ballroom, the Futurist Theatre, the 'Theatre in the Round', band concerts, firework displays, dances, discos, bingo for members and guests at the Mecca Centre.

Sporting activities provide an equally lengthy list: both coarse and sea fishing, boating, bowling, tennis, county cricket matches and the seven-day September Festival; national and international motor cycle racing on Oliver's Mount, skin-diving and waterskiing.

As to history, it seems certain that an Iron Age settlement existed on the same site.Then the Romans established a coastal signal station on the Castle Headland almost two millennia ago. According to legend, around AD 966 an individual named Skarthi, meaning 'scarface', founded the town itself. Laid waste in Viking raids, it was only after 1127, under the protection of the Norman Castle which gave Castle Headland its name, that the town began to grow again.

At the time of the English Civil War, Scarborough was eventually the only Royalist port on the east coast and was besieged by Cromwell himself, finally capitulating to Parliament in 1645. Oliver's Mount was named after him and is today clearly identified by its 21 metres (75 ft) high war memorial. Much later the castle was still in use as a place of detention. Scarborough Castle last saw action as recently as 1914 when it was bombarded and partially destroyed by the German fleet.

The life and economy of the town have always been linked to the sea but prosperity came in 1626 with the discovery of mineral medicinal spring waters. By the middle of the C17th, the curative powers of these spring waters were so well-known that many people had visited the town to partake of their excellent qualities. When sea bathing too became fashionable in the early C18th, new and often grand houses were built. In 1827 the Spa Bridge opened as a toll bridge and soon the 'Spa Buildings' became a social centre. With the opening of the York - Scarborough Railway in 1845, the large urban populations of Yorkshire could visit, and business boomed. The population soared from 13,000 to 33,000 in only 40 years.

A sea wall constructed around the Castle Headland in 1908 became the Marine Drive and a splendid sea-front walk and drive, but Scarborough has not lost its links with the fishing industry. In 1952, the harbour was deepened to allow the entry of vessels up to 1000 tonnes.

Of the many interesting buildings in the town, we must mention the Town Hall, Grand Hotel, Market Hall and St Mary's Church, the burial place of Anne Bronte, which is C12th in origin. There are also several interesting museums to enjoy. In addition, St Martin's Church, built in 1862, was richly decorated by William Morris and other members of the Pre-Raphaelite Brotherhood.

SCARBOROUGH IS PARTICULARLY RICH IN PARKS AND GARDENS. On the South Cliff are the Shuttleworth Gardens, specially designed for blind visitors with fragrant plants, and plant labels in braille. Meandering paths lead down through the famous Holbeck and Italian Gardens designed by Sir Joseph Paxton (the creator of the famous gardens of Chatsworth in Derbyshire) past the Belvedere Rose Gardens and eventually to the Spa Gardens. The Gardens of Northstead Manor and Peasholm Park both have positions overlooking the North Bay. At Northstead Manor Gardens, children can enjoy boating, a miniature railway and Mavel's Fun Park (a Disneyland-style entertainment imported from the USA). Nearby, for younger children, there is Kinderland, a fun, play and activity park.

At Peasholm Park, the beautiful Valley Gardens display many exotic shrubs and trees and the lake has island pagodas and waterfalls. Twice weekly, the lake resounds to the sound of fireworks as great naval battles are re-enacted here. Further along the Esplanade, the Alexandra Gardens offer peaceful illuminated walks at night.

Long Distance Walks

The area of the North York Moors and Coast has an enormous amount to offer the long distance walker, both in miles of trails available and in the variety of countryside through which they pass. The **Cleveland Way** (93 miles - 150km) is the longest, and includes a long stretch of coastal walking. The **North Yorkshire Moors Crosses Walk** (54 miles - 90km), the **Lyke Wake Walk** (40 miles - 65km), and the **White Rose Walk** (37 miles - 60km) all traverse moorland, while the **Missing Link** (50 miles - 80km) brings the Cleveland Way full circle, and the more modest Forestry Commission **Long Distance Trail** (16 miles - 26km) makes use of the region's forests.

THE CLEVELAND WAY was the second long distance footpath to be established by the Countryside Commission. Opening in May 1969, the walk started at Helmsley, moved north along the western escarpment to Roseberry Topping, continued north-east to the coast at Saltburn and then followed the cliffs south to end near Filey. The route is signposted and waymarked with the **acorn symbol**, and should normally be undertaken and enjoyed in some 10 to 14 days. In 1975, the ends of the 'Way' were joined by the Missing Link walk, from Crook Ness on the coast to Helmsley.

THE NORTH YORKSHIRE MOORS CROSSES WALK is officially held every July, starting and finishing at Goathland. In the course of the walk, some thirteen moorland crosses are passed.

THE LYKE WAKE WALK is perhaps the best known of the walks in the area. It was established by **Bill Cowley** in 1955 and since that time has been completed by over 80,000 people. The object is to complete the course in under 24 hours, but the fastest crossing was in around 5 hours. Another strange fact is that several people have done the walk about 150 times! The name 'Lyke Wake' is derived from the ancient **Cleveland Lyke Wake Dirge** which suggested that after death, the soul would make a journey over the moors. 'Lyke' means corpse and 'Wake' the watching over the corpse. The route starts at **Osmotherley** on the western edge of the North York Moors, and follows the watershed eastward to end at **Ravenscar** on the Yorkshire coast. Actually, the 'official' start and finish points are a little away from these villages on foot, making the

distance to be walked quite a bit further than 40 miles. Not only is this the widest part of the moors; there is some 1500 metres (5000ft) of climbing! Make sure that you are physically prepared as well as possessing the proper equipment. So popular has this walk become that there is a very large **Lyke Wake Club.**

THE WHITE ROSE WALK takes its name from the two landmarks which it links, namely **Roseberry Topping** and the **White Horse.** It was established in 1968 and has steadily grown in popularity. One unusual feature is that in the middle of the walk there are three alternative sections to follow. These provide variation for those who undertake the walk more than once, but also affect its length which can be either 34, 37 or 40 miles.

THE FORESTRY COMMISSION LONG DISTANCE TRAIL is a waymarked route through forests, from **Reasty Bank** above **Harwood Dale** to **Allerston** at the edge of the **Vale of Pickering.**

On reflection, there seems to have been a boom in the development of walks. Others include the six **Esk Valley Walkways** from stations along the Esk Valley Line; **the Historical Railway Trail** between Grosmont and Goathland, both stations on the North York Moors Railway; and the new **Century Way** from Filey to York.

Mention must be made of the path along the **track-bed of the old Scarborough to Whitby Railway,** from the outskirts of Scarborough to Hawsker, which is north of Robin Hood's Bay and only a few miles south of Whitby. This track, now known as **the 'Trailway',** was purchased by Scarborough District Council for recreational purposes and can be used by the public for cycling and riding as well as walking.

Finally, **a note of caution:** walkers on the coastal routes should take particular care, especially in winter when thick mists, locally known as 'roaks', can descend, making it hard to navigate and also very cold. After prolonged rain, landslips are more likely, and this is another hazard. Sturdy footwear, sensible clothes and emergency rations are essential, and **none but the most experienced walkers** should tackle any of the long walks, whether on the coast or the moors.

Also remember that climbing up and down hills or steep paths is much slower than walking on the flat, so allow yourself extra time. And **always notify someone else** of your intended route and expected time of arrival, so that, if you do get into difficulties, help should soon be on its way.

Captain Cook Country Heritage Trail

James Cook's **international reknown** brings many thousands of visitors to find out more about the man and the area in which he lived.

His fame began in 1759, at the age of 31, when he successfully charted the very difficult waters of the **St Lawrence River,** thus enabling **General Wolfe** to conquer the **'Heights of Abraham'** and **Quebec,** and claim **Canada** as a British possession. Then the high quality of Cook's reports from his first naval command impressed members of the **Royal Society** back in Britain. This led to Cook's first great voyage. In 1768 in the Whitby-built **'Endeavour',** he set out to enable the **Royal Society** to monitor a **transit of Venus** from **Tahiti,** the best observation point, and to **chart the southern Pacific** on behalf of the Admiralty.

Cook charted New Zealand, then moved on to the east coast of **Australia** to land at a place so rich in plants and wildlife that the delighted scientists named it **Botany Bay.** Claiming the land for **George III,** Cook submitted a report which engendered the idea that convicts could serve their sentences there. This led, 20 years later, to the settlement of Australia, when the first shipload of 100 people, mostly convicts, established a settlement at **Port Jackson,** now known as **Sydney.**

Cook's next, three-year voyage, in the 'Resolution' in 1772, was to seek the reported 'southern continent'. Although unsuccessful, he discovered many lands, including **Easter Island** and huge areas of **Antarctica,** before returning around the tip of **South America** and across the Atlantic. For his achievements, he was elected **Fellow of the Royal Society,** and appointed **Captain of Greenwich Hospital.**

His third expedition, to locate a north-west passage from the Atlantic to the Pacific, left England in 1776, again with the **'Resolution',** and a new ship **'Discovery'.** Much valuable surveying was undertaken but no such passage was discovered. In 1779, James Cook was killed in a skirmish with natives on the **Sandwich Islands,** now known as **Hawaii.**

The **'Heritage Trail'** was established in 1978, the **250th anniversary** of Cook's birth. It gives the visitor an intimate glimpse into the background and life of an extraordinary man, both sailor and scientist, who said of himself that he 'had the ambition not only to go further than any man had ever been before, but as far as it was possible for man to go'.

MARTON Here, The Captain Cook Birthplace Museum in Stewart Park features Cook's life and travels; and a magnificent conservatory displays plants typical of those brought back from Cook's voyages by Joseph Banks and other botanists. A granite vase marks the site of the small thatched cottage where he was born in 1728, the second of eight children, only three of whom survived to adulthood. Marton Parish Church register still records his baptism in 1728. A stone monument from Point Hicks, the first Australian land sighted by Cook, is on the village green.

GREAT AYTON James Cook's farm labourer father worked for a time at Airyholme Farm below nearby Roseberry Topping. His employer was Mr. Thomas Skottowe, at Ayton Hall (now a hotel). The site of the cottage in which the Cook family later lived (now in Fitzroy Gardens, Melbourne) is marked by a granite memorial. Part of the building in which the young James Cook went to school is now the Captain Cook Schoolroom Museum. The old parish churchyard at Great Ayton contains the Cook family tombstone, marking the grave of his mother and five of his brothers and sisters.

EASBY MOOR Not far away is the site of a fine monument to Cook, erected in 1827.

MARSKE Only the tower remains of St Germain's Church, demolished in 1960. Cook's father and sister were buried nearby.

STAITHES When Cook left school he worked for a time on the farm, then in a general dealer's shop in the fishing village of Staithes, since washed into the sea; salvaged parts may have been incorporated into what a Heritage Trail plaque declares as Cook's Cottage.

WHITBY In the shipyards where the 'Endeavour', 'Resolution' and 'Discovery' were built as colliers, Cook proved an avid student of navigation and later chose these stable, wide-bottomed collier vessels for his great voyages of exploration. Despite rapid promotion on the Walker Brothers' ships and the offer of the captaincy of his own ship, he chose to enlist in the Royal Navy. Whitby Museum has a revolving globe showing the routes of Cook's voyages and many other exhibits; The Captain Cook Memorial Museum occupies John Walker's house in Grape Lane and also has fascinating displays; and there is a bronze statue by John Tweed on the West Cliff, showing Cook gazing over the bay where his seafaring began.

Drive One
Western Circular
60 miles (96km)

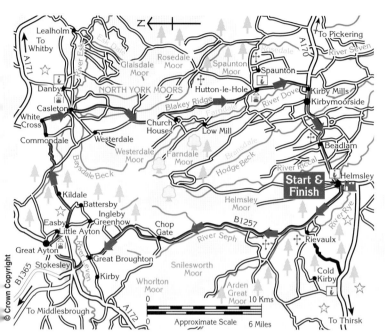

ROUTE:

This is a demanding drive, needing time to do justice to many interesting sites en route.

Leave **Helmsley Market Place**, pass the church, and travel on the B1257 to **Stokesley**. Climb along the edge of **Duncombe Park**, the grounds of which are open to the public. There is, after two miles, a worthwhile diversion to **Rievaulx village and Abbey.**

The Forestry Commission car park, with picnic places, viewing platform and toilets, is on the right as you approach the escarpment at **Newgate Bank**. The steep descent into the valley below takes you past farms with names that evoke the great monastic sheep-rearing days: Woolhouse Croft, Ewe Cote and Wether Cote. Next to the Sun Inn, look out for Spout House, a C16th cruck-framed thatched house, with C17th windows, that was the local inn until the Sun Inn took over in 1914.

From the settlement of **Chop Gate**, referred to locally as 'Chop Yat', continue uphill to the nick through which the road crosses the moorland watershed. Two famous long distance walks cross the road here: the Cleveland Way and the Lyke Wake Walk. The car park at the top of **Clay Bank** has an excellent view towards Middlesbrough and the conical hill called Roseberry Topping. Continue along the main road through **Broughton**, and turn right at the roundabout for **Great Ayton**, an attractive village associated with Captain Cook .

Just this side of the bridge into the village, take the road to **Easby** and **Kildale**, which provides fine views behind to Roseberry Topping and to the Captain Cook Monument on Easby Moor. After two miles, turn towards **Kildale**. After Kildale Hall, a late Georgian or early Edwardian building, the road keeps company with the **Esk Valley Railway**. The line

was constructed in sections: this link between Stokesley and Castleton opened in 1861.

Four miles beyond Kildale, we come to **Commondale**. Despite its name, this place is unique in appearance: its houses are built, not from stones, but from red and yellow bricks manufactured at the local brickworks, established in 1861.

Climbing steeply onto the open moorlands, turn right at **White Cross**, which is reached after one mile. Another steep descent leads down to the River Esk. Cross by the bridge, built in 1873 to replace a medieval bow bridge. Bear left for the village of **Castleton**, which, as the name suggests, once boasted a castle, built in 1089. At the top of the hill, the road skirts the large mound which is all that remains of the Norman defences.

Turn right at the junction for **Hutton-le-Hole**. The road passes through **Castleton** and climbs up **Castleton Rigg**, with excellent views into Danby Dale on the left. Climbing higher, there are enjoyable routes to the right into Westerdale. **Ralph Cross**, or 'Young Ralph', replaces a C13th stone cross on the same site, which marks the highest point of 1400 ft (426 metres). Old Ralph is a much smaller stone cross 200 metres to the west.

Descend into **Hutton-le-Hole**, turn left at the first junction, and stop in the car park. This stone-built village has wide-open greens, sheep grazing, and a stream passing through its centre. Notice the ancient pinfold where stray animals were impounded by the village pindar until a fine was paid. Visit the Ryedale Folk Museum, with exhibits that depict life in the area through the centuries.

Three miles south of here, the road meets the A170 at **Kirkby Mills**. Turn right for your destination, **Helmsley**.

Drive Two
Eastern Circular
53 miles (85km)

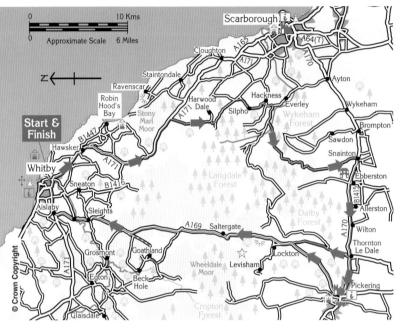

This is part of Lord Derwent's estate, with his Hall, built in 1791. Visit the church at Hackness, then follow the road round the lake, which is part of the landscaping of the Hall.

At the war memorial, go straight ahead towards **Broxa** and **Langdale End**, turning left at the first junction. Cross the River Derwent and the Hilla Green Bridge, and follow the valley between **Wykeham Forest** to the left, and **Bickley Forest** on the right.

At **Manor House**, the road, once only a track between isolated farms, passes through a farmyard. Climb to the summit at the head of the valley for magnificent views, along with ancient earthworks, great banks and ditches thought by some to have been field boundaries or animal pounds.

Follow generally downhill to **Stainton** along the limestones to the flat expanse of the **Vale of Pickering**. Reach the A170, and turn right to either **Thornton Dale** or **Pickering**, where another right turn will lead back to **Whitby**. The two routes meet at the Fox and Rabbit Inn, which has its own domestic windmill.

On the right after 4 miles, there is a car park with a large National Park board. Opposite and to the left is the unusual **Hole of Horcum**. Along with nearby Levisham Moor, this area is noted for its rare flora and early remains.

Further on, there are excellent views from the escarpment towards Newtondale and Fylindales Moors, which are managed for sheep and grouse. Over to the right were once sited the three great white spheres of the Fylingdales Early Warning Station, now replaced by the 'pyramid', while at the head of Newtondale is the nature reserve of Fen Bog.

A detour will take you to **Goathland**, but descend to **Sleights** from **Sil Howe**. Climb to the junction with A171 and turn right for **Whitby**.

ROUTE:

A drive through the moors, which can be attempted from **Whitby**, **Scarborough** or **Pickering**.

Leaving **Whitby** on the A171 Scarborough road, climb onto the moorlands. Drive towards **Hawsker**, alongside the trackbed of the Scarborough-Whitby Railway, a splendid line which since its closure has been used for walks.

Leave **Hawsker**, where there is an unusual church tower, and complete the climb onto the moorlands. You will see the Esk Valley, and the flat-topped hill known as Blakey Topping. A mile after passing the **Flask Inn,** there are traces of the old road with fine views of the steeply-rising Tabular Hills. This spot is also an important point for Lyke Wake Walk support teams, as it is the last road crossing on the 40 mile walk, and marks the '3 miles to go' to the finish at the radio mast at

Ravenscar.

A local curiosity from the hollows of nearby Stoney Marl Moor, drained by Helwath Beck, is a bog moss called sphagnum, collected as lining for hanging flower baskets!

Take the first road on the right, leading to **Harwood Dale.** The ruins of Harwood Dale Chapel of 1634 can be seen a short distance past Chapel Farm, but lie on private land.

The route veers right and climbs steeply towards **Silpho** and **Hackness**. At the summit is a car park with a panoramic view across Harwood Dale. If you wish to stretch your legs, there is a 3 mile forest trail from here.

At **Turkey Carpet**, there is a choice of routes. A right turn will lead through **Silpho** with its excellent views but dangerous hairpin bends. For an easier route, go straight ahead, providing fine views over Scarborough before you descend into **Hackness Valley.**

Walk One
Staithes
3.5 miles (5km)

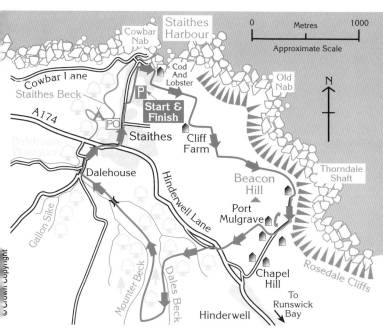

permits (the walk can be rejoined afterwards by way of **Runswick Lane** and Hinderwell).

ROUTE INSTRUCTIONS:

From the old railway car park, on the right of the main street down to the harbour, turn right and walk downhill. This is the oldest part of Staithes. On the right, beyond the 'Cod and Lobster', you will find a narrow street, typical of Staithes in the old days.

Go down this, and you will pass the house where, it is claimed, Cook lived whilst working in Staithes. Soon after this, climb up the cliff along the coast path, via the steps.

Continue until you come to a farm, and soon you will be crossing open fields a little inland. This part of the path is a section of the Cleveland Way, and is therefore well-signposted. After half a mile you come to the cliff edge. Being extremely careful follow this along below Beacon Hill to Port Mulgrave. It is at this point that you can continue on to Runswick Bay if you so choose.

From Port Mulgrave, turn right at the lane, away from the sea. Turn right between houses once belonging to harbour officials, opposite the telephone box on your left. Beyond the houses, bear left for 400 metres, and cross the A174 to a small slip road (a little to the left), and descend to the woods following the yellow arrows. In the wood, turn left onto the footbridge over Dales Beck. Follow the path uphill to a junction on the right.

Walk to the gate at the end of the wood, cross the field to a belt of trees, then descend steeply to the bridge by the caravan site. The lane over the bridge leads to the road. Continue to the A174 and turn right and then almost immediately left to the main thoroughfare of Staithes.

ROUTE:

The walk is a very easy stroll which starts and finishes at the **old railway car park** in **Staithes** (approach on the A174), then threads its way among the houses until it reaches the cliff path. Follow this until it comes to the tiny harbour of **Port Mulgrave**, then walk away from the sea into the tiny 'hidden' valley of **Borrowby Dale**, containing **Dales Beck.** Go over the footbridge, up to the gate at the end of the wood, and turn right into **Staithes.** It should take no more than two and a half hours, even allowing for exploration and even pausing to enjoy the splendid views.

GENERAL DESCRIPTION:

Nestling on the steep sides of a valley where it opens onto the North Sea, **Staithes** is a gem among villages. **Captain James Cook** was apprenticed to a general dealer here, and the village is proud of the connection.

However, a few years after Cook left Staithes for the next stage of his career in **Whitby**, the actual premises where he worked were washed into the sea by North Sea storms - a not uncommon occurrence along this coastline which has gradually retreated over the centuries. Some buildings still remain, albeit much rebuilt, from Cook's lifetime, notably the 'Cod and Lobster' pub.

Above Staithes lie the cliffs, and, from **Beacon Hill**, there are extensive views into the moorlands on a fine day. Below Beacon Hill is **Port Mulgrave.** This was once a busy port for iron ore, which was brought along a narrow-gauge railway to the coast for shipment, having been mined around Boulby.

However, with its heyday far in the past, Port Mulgrave is now small and forgotten, and therefore ripe for rediscovery. **Runswick Bay** lies further along the cliffs, and is well worth a visit if time

Walk Two
Hole of Horcum
2.5 miles (4km)

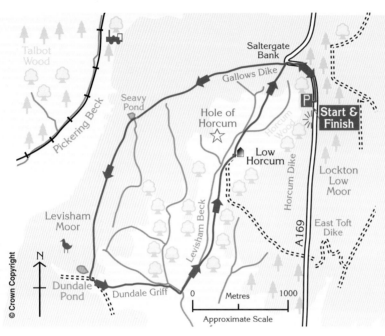

© Crown Copyright

ROUTE:

This short walk, rich in landscape and wildlife, starts and finishes at the car park above **Saltergate Bank** off the A169, 8 miles north of Pickering. Pass the **Hole of Horcum** on the left, and walk down along **the Devil's Elbow** and **Gallow's Dyke,** taking in the impressive views into Saltergate, Fylingdales and **Newtondale.** Go on to Levisham Moor, find **Seavy Pond,** and then go on to **Dundale Pond** and back via **Low Horcum.**

GENERAL DESCRIPTION:

The **moorlands** above Pickering are attractive at any time of year, but particularly so in August and early September, when the **heather** is in bloom. The tiny flowers blossom in late August, covering the moors with a **purple carpet** which, on closer inspection, provides a spectrum from whites, pinks and mauves to deepest purple.

Each square mile of moorland produces **three million flowers** each year, which in turn produce quantities of seed.

Heather moorland constitutes almost half the National Park, and is managed as a habitat for **red grouse** (a dark reddish-brown game bird the size of a small chicken). It flies low over the heather with a rapid wing beat followed by a glide, calling out 'go-bak, bak-bak-bak'. Other birds you may see are the **meadow pipit, skylark, curlew** and **kestrel.**

The first sight on your walk, the **Hole of Horcum,** is a huge basin created by springs seeping between the sandstone and clay halfway down the hillside. The contrast between the vegetation on the upper and lower slopes indicates the effect that the underlying rock has on the soil. **Legend** has it that **a giant** called Wade grabbed up a handful of earth to throw at his wife in a fit of anger, thus leaving the Hole, and creating a new hill -

Blakey Topping. An avalanche during one of the almost arctic winters is said to have damaged the farmhouse in the Hole beyond repair.

Newtondale is a tremendous gash in the landscape, cut by overflow from a glacial lake fifteen thousand years ago. It is a natural routeway across the moors, and **George Stephenson** engineered the railway along it.

Near **Seavy Pond,** a small pool (sometimes dry) in a clay-lined hollow, there are three **Bronze Age tumuli** (burial mounds) on **Levisham Moor.**

Other archaeological sites on the Moor span a period of three and a half thousand years: further on is an **Iron Age Dyke,** a two millenia-old ditch banked on both sides; thought to have delineated territory for farmers (remains of a farm lie nearby).

Dundale Pond and Griff are the next beauty spots on your walk, which heads towards the farm at **Low Horcum,** and then turns for home.

ROUTE INSTRUCTIONS:

Cross the road from the car park, and follow downhill to the sharp bend in the road. On your left is the Hole of Horcum (or 'the Devil's Punchbowl'). Walk onto the Devil's Elbow, where the way drops to the lower moor from the road.

Within a mile of the A169, you will reach Seavy Pond. From the bank above you can see the Bronze Age Barrows and Levisham Moor. Continue on to pass the Iron Age Dyke.

Carry on to Dundale Pond, on the right of the path. Turn left here, and pass Dundale Griff. Bear left after a while, cross the footbridge, and follow the left-pointing yellow arrow, beside the stream.

Cross the stile and climb the bank up to the farm building at Low Horcum. With this on your right, follow the yellow arrow over a stile, and go steeply uphill to the A169. Turn right towards the car park.

Walk Three
Farndale
3.75 miles (5.75km)

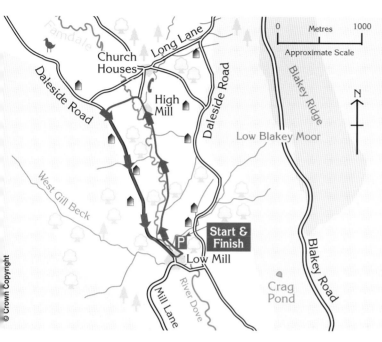

ROUTE:

This gentle amble starts and finishes at **Low Mill.** Follow along the **River Dove** until you reach **High Mill**, a disused corn mill set among daffodils. Pass by, and you will reach **Church Houses,** where there is a thatched cottage, or turn left for **Cow Bank.** Turn left again, and you can return along the road.

GENERAL DESCRIPTION:

There are no long views on this walk, because the dale is hemmed in by the high moorland of **Blakey Ridge** to the east and **Rudland Rigg** to the west. However, their presence is not overpowering, as the dale is quite wide, and provides a pleasant rural setting for a stroll.

The **River Dove,** which flows through the dale, took its name from the Celtic word 'dubo', which means shady stream. This is apt, because from its source at the head of the valley of **Farndale** to its

confluence with the **River Rye,** it is bordered by wooded and shady banks.

Farndale's name is more obscure, but perhaps harks back to the time when the valley was densely wooded with trees such as the alder, whose **Gaelic name** is 'ferna'. These trees, with round-ended leaves and small cone-like female catkins, may still be seen along the riverbank.

There are many flowers to be found in Farndale, but the valley is chiefly famous for its 'host of **golden daffodils'.** These flowers are so often associated with Wordsworth and the Lake District that it is often almost forgotten that they grow in other areas at all.

However, putting paid to this delusion, the vale of Farndale is busiest in **April,** when visitors venture here to appreciate the beauties of the multitude of wild daffodils. It is thought that the monks of **Rievaulx Abbey** introduced the daffodils to the valley in the

C12th and C13th, although some people attribute them to a C17th Roman Catholic priest, sowing them as a silent protest at the religious persecution and prejudice he met with in England.

Whatever its provenance, this gift of nature is so popular that the picking of flowers by visitors has become a problem. This grew to such serious proportions that a local **Nature Reserve** was established in 1955 to provide full protection. Furthermore, during the daffodil season, the National Park Warden Service operates from a caravan at **Low Mill**, offering advice and a 'caring eye': so be nice: don't have a 'roving hand', but leave the flowers there for others to enjoy, as the monks or the Roman Catholic priest would have wanted.

The greatest concentration of daffodils is around **High Mill.** Here you will see steep Liassic shale cliffs, masked on the valley floor by glacial (ice) and alluvial (river) deposits, and constantly eroded by the river.

Ironstone is also found in the valley. The poor quality of the ore prevented large-scale exploitation, though a railway carried ironstone to Middlesbrough round the head of the valley in the C19th.

ROUTE INSTRUCTIONS:

Leave from the corner of the car park opposite the Post Office at Low Mill, (12 miles north of Kirkbymoorside). Study the map and information board. Cross the river by the footbridge, and follow the riverside path to High Mill, where you pass through the yard to a signpost pointing ahead to Church Houses, or turn left up Cow Bank. If you do, you can turn left along the road to get back. Otherwise retrace your footsteps.

It is worth noting that the valley operates a one-way road system during the peak daffodil season, in order to cope with the volume of traffic and ease congestion.

Walk Four
Sutton Bank & The White Horse
2 miles (3.25km)

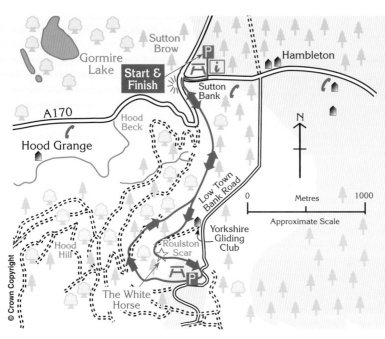

© Crown Copyright

ROUTE:

The walk starts and finishes in the car park at **Sutton Bank**, where there is a picnic site and **National Park Information Centre**, with a cafe and also an accommodation booking facility. Walk along the escarpment top past **Lake Gormire** until you reach **the White Horse of Kilburn**. Return via the lower track.

GENERAL DESCRIPTION:

The White Horse of Kilburn is familiar to travellers on the railway between **York** and **Darlington**. The figure is immense: 324ft (96 metres) from head to tail and 228ft (70 metres) high. It was cut in 1857 by the village schoolmaster, **Thomas Taylor**, and thirty helpers, the outline having been staked out on the hillside. Unlike in southern England, where similar figures were cut in white chalk, Taylor painted it with gallons of **whitewash**, and it could be seen for miles. Over the years, however, it deteriorated until a committee of local people was founded to restore and maintain the Horse. Today, **chalk chippings** from the Yorkshire Wolds are used instead of whitewash.

Other attractions on this walk are more natural: **Lake Gormire**, for example, is traditionally said to be **bottomless** because many springs from the adjacent slopes feed water into the lake, but there is no apparent outlet for the water. In fact, it seeps underground to emerge as a spring about a mile away.

The escarpment top above Lake Gormire supports masses of **wild bilberry** plants, and a few, isolated trees that clearly show the effects of the dominant wind. It was here, in 1332, that the **Battle of Byland** was fought between the armies of **Edward II of England** and **Robert the Bruce of Scotland**. The escarpment is now used by the **Yorkshire Gliding Club**, which was established here in 1931.

Nearby **Hood Hill** is the site of a castle probably built by Robert de Stuteville around 1086; and the remains of the motte and bailey can be seen.

Close by is the site of a Cistercian cell founded in 1138, but occupied for only five years by the abbot and twelve monks who eventually founded Byland Abbey in 1177. Finally, **Roulston Scar** at the corner of the Escarpment displays the warm creamy-coloured gritstone frequently used as local building stone.

It is worth noting that there are plenty of other walks around **Sutton Bank**: look out for the National Park booklet 'Family Walks around Sutton Bank', available from the **Sutton Bank Visitor Centre**, for further information.

ROUTE INSTRUCTIONS:

Cross the main road from the car park to the top of the escarpment. You will see Lake Gormire below to the right, at the foot of the bank. Take the left path along the edge of the escarpment, which takes you past the Yorkshire Gliding Club on your left. Take great care, particularly if children are with you. Over to your right is Hood Hill, outlying from the main escarpment. Continuing on, you reach the White Horse. For those who do not wish to make the descent and ascent needed to complete a circular tour, you should retrace your footsteps from this point. If you are more energetic, descend the steps by the White Horse (please do not step on the chalk, as this speeds erosion), at the bottom of the steps turn right and follow a track, cross the car park, and follow a track along the foot of the escarpment before climbing the diagonal path on the right, known as the Thief's Highway. This brings you back to your earlier pathway at the top, where you bear left for the Sutton Bank car park.

Walk Five
Captain Cook Country
1.5 or 4 miles (0.5 or 6.5km)

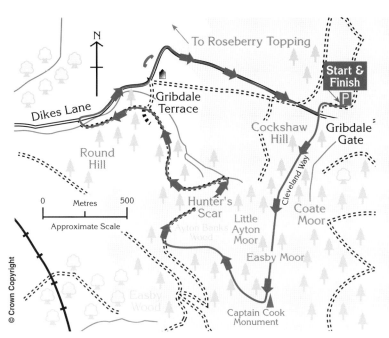

ROUTE:

The walk starts and finishes at **Gribdale Gate car park,** leads uphill to the **Cook Monument.** The route goes downhill towards **Roseberry Topping,** along the foot of **Larner's Hill,** and follows the narrow lane up to **Gribdale Terrace,** and then up the bank to **Gribdale Gate** again.

GENERAL DESCRIPTION:

Captain Cook who was born at Marton, was in this neighbourhood, on the 27th October 1728, according to the monument. This sturdy looking sandstone edifice dates from 1827. It looks out to **Roseberry Topping** and **Airey Holme Farm** where Cook spent his early years. **Great Ayton,** the village where Cook attended school is also clearly visible from the monument. In the opposite direction, there is a view down the western escarpment of the **Cleveland Hills,** while to the west, the Northern Pennines rise from

the flat vale of the Tees.

This area has been mined very extensively, as you see when you look at the landscape: **Roseberry Topping,** for example, was originally a conical hill, prior to 1873, when drift mines opened along its lower slopes in order to extract ironstone. Mining operations led to landslips, which still occur, though the mines ceased to operate in 1929.

The great scar of **Cliff Ridge Wood** is additional evidence of the extractive industry in the area. The stone from here was a hard volcanic basalt or whinstone, in demand as a roadstone during the C19th and early C20th.

At the bottom of **Larner's Hill,** you will see the old trackbed of a railway branch line of the **Whitby to Middlesbrough railway,** which can also be seen nearby. It had to work on a steep gradient, dropping 137 metres over a distance of only 275

metres! This, though, was not a victim of the infamous Beecham railway closures: it only existed to carry the fruit of the mines further on, and when they closed, the branch line went with them.

With all this industry, people would have to be housed, and we find a single terrace of houses, built in the C19th for the ironstone miners, at **Gribdale Terrace.** It is an unusual sight, and a moving symbol of the way in which industry has habitually transplanted people to alien and sometimes harsh environments throughout the centuries. At least now the houses have a good view to look out over: before, they might have gazed across on a landscape torn up by mining.

Slightly further on from here, **Gribdale Gate** itself explains the lonely presence of the terraced houses: this area of hillside has seen the greatest diversity of mining and quarrying of anywhere in the North York Moors. Alum shale was quarried between 1765 and 1771, jet was worked for a very brief period around 1840, and building stone, ironstone and whinstone were cut from quarries at the top of the bank over many years.

ROUTE INSTRUCTIONS:

From the Gribdale Gate car park, follow the broad path uphill between coniferous trees, until you reach the Cook Monument. This is part of the Cleveland Way. Retrace your footsteps for the short walk. For the longer walk, cross diagonally downhill towards Roseberry Topping, into a conifer plantation. At the end, the path follows the stone wall, then turns sharp right down a track to the lane up to the Great Ayton to Gribdale road. Turn right up the lane to reach Gribdale Terrace. Pass in front of the Terrace, and continue straight ahead up the bank, which is Gribdale Gate.

Walk Six
Falling Foss
2.9 miles (4.7km)

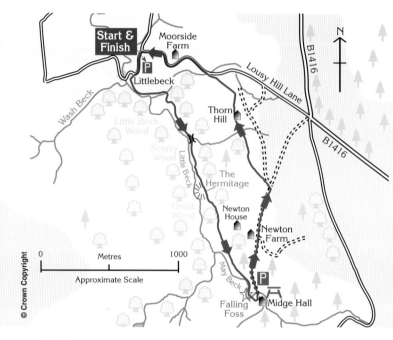

ROUTE:

This challenging walk wends its way in and around the forest. To get there, take the B1416 off the A171 (the Whitby to Scarborough Road) to **Littlebeck**. Negotiate the steep drop to the stream, which you cross. Climb the steps to the stone hollow of **the Hermitage**, downhill once more until you reach **Falling Foss waterfall**. Then retrace your footsteps to the bridge over the stream, and head uphill to the right past a farm and into the wonderfully-named **Lousy Hill Lane**, before turning left to reach your destination.

GENERAL DESCRIPTION:

Falling Foss is one of the most beautiful of the Yorkshire waterfalls. Its strange name may come from the Old English word 'fosse', meaning a narrow ditch or stream - no great tribute to the power of the water here!

And indeed, the waterfalls of the North York Moors are not large, as in other places in the country, but they make up in beauty what they lack in size. Many of them, with evocative names such as **Water Ark, Thomason Foss** and **Mallyan Spout** (the highest of the waterfalls), are close together on the **West Beck** in the **Murk Esk Valley near Goathland.**

Falling Foss, on the other hand, is some way away from the others, on **Little Beck**, a different tributary of the **River Esk**. Here the water rolls over moss-covered rocks before tumbling into a dark pool below. The rocks are said by legend to be the hoary heads of **a coven of witches,** turned to stone and swallowed by the stream as they tried to cross the water in pursuit of a boy named Thomas, who had seen them at their wicked work one full moon. Where they lie half-buried, the stream runs in triumph over their heads: witches cannot cross running water, so you are safe as long as Falling Foss continues to flow - but the same legend warns that, should the stream ever run dry, the witches will rise groaning from their centuries-old sleep and go shrieking in pursuit of the first living thing to meet their eyes.

Another curious thing on the walk is **the Hermitage,** carved by a stonemason named Jeffrey in the year 1790. Perhaps he had it in his head to provide shelter for lovers, for the dark hollow of the Hermitage hides two stone seats. It is certainly a good place to admire the view.

ROUTE INSTRUCTIONS:

Take the road downhill from the car park. Turn left, and follow the public footpath sign. The drop down to the stream is steep here. Cross the stream by the bridge, and climb the steps just before the small cave.

Follow the path as it wanders along, and soon cross over a small stone wall. Two hundred metres later, climb the steps, and you will see the Hermitage at the top where you can pause and enjoy the view. From here take the left fork in the path. Follow the yellow arrow down the small steps, and turn right where the path splits. Continue downhill and you will reach Falling Foss waterfall. Take the path on the right by Midge Hall and descend onto the stones above the Fall for a different view - but it is important that caution is taken. From here, retrace your steps to the bridge, and follow the path uphill to the right of the path you first came along. Find the bridleway, pass the farm on your left, and turn left at the public footpath sign.

Carry on over rough ground past two buildings on the left, then onto a dirt track to the right, and you will reach Lousy Hill Lane. Turn left and follow the road downhill back to the car park.

North York Moors & Coast in Colour - A Personal Collection

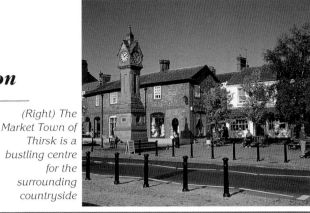

(Right) The Market Town of Thirsk is a bustling centre for the surrounding countryside

(Above) The broad greens in the pretty village of Hutton-le-Hole are an appealing characteristic

(Right) The quaint stone-built cottages in Lockton are typical of many of the pretty little villages of the area

(Below) Thornton-le-Dale is thought by many people to be one of Yorkshire's prettiest villages

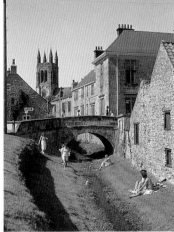

(Above) This peaceful scene in one of Helmsley's hidden corners typifies the delights to be discovered with a little exploration

(Below) The towering keep of Helmsley Castle is a prominent landmark

(Above) The extensive remains of Helmsley Castle provide a variety of architectural interest

(Right) A seaward view from the imposing remains of Whitby Abbey

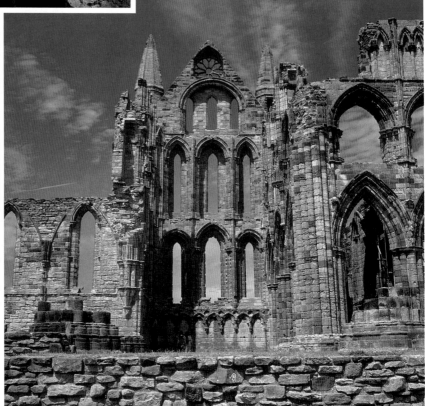

(Above) The famous landmark of Captain Cook's Monument on the purple Easby Moor

(Right) The majestic ruins of the famous Whitby Abbey

(Left) The imposing gateway to the impressive Scarborough Castle

(Below) The setting of Rievaulx Abbey is as beautiful as the remains themselves

(Above) Rievaulx Temples and Terrace offer a splendid viewpoint over the Abbey below

(Above) The magnificent remains of Pickering's motte and bailey castle are well worth a visit

(Right) The tiny historic chapel in the grounds of Pickering Castle

(Left) A characteristic stone cross on the heather-clad Kildale Moor

(Above) Quiet country lanes enable visitors to explore the unspoilt expanses of Commondale Moor

(Right) The famous Ralph Cross on the moorland panorama of Westerdale Moor

(Below) A blanket of purple heather on Kildale Moor is a beautiful characteristic of the region

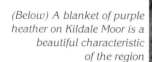

(Below) The famous White Cross on Danby High Moor

(Below) Another ancient stone cross on Kildale Moor

(Right) Beautiful green dales such as Rosedale separate the heather clad moors

(Below) This extensive panorama over Eskdale's broad, green, rural expanse is one of many fine views to be enjoyed

(Below) The famous wild daffodils that adorn Farndale are one of the region's exquisite attractions

(Above) Looking towards the famous Sutton Bank viewpoint

(Below) Solitary grousebutts on Rosedale Moor typify the remoteness and isolation of this unspoilt region

(Right) Looking from the pretty village of Great Ayton towards the famous landmark summit of Roseberry Topping

(Right) Sandcastles on Scarborough beach display an age-old pastime for young and old

(Above) A peaceful scene looking over the fishing boats in pretty Runswick Bay

(Right) A tremendous view over the busy fishing harbour at Scarborough to the lofty castle beyond

(Below) Donkey rides are a traditional seaside pastime - seen here at Scarborough's South Bay

(Left) These lobster pots display the fishing tradition at Runswick Bay

(Left) The peaceful and beautiful shoreline at Staithes

(Above) A splendid panorama looking northwards over the quaint settlements of Staithes and Cowbar

(Right) The almost fairy-tale setting and appeal of the ever-popular Robin Hood's Bay

(Below) Another breathtaking panorama over Cowbar and Staithes - this time looking southwards

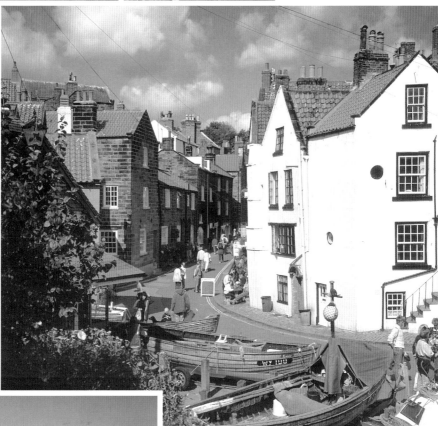

(Right) The small beck between Staithes and Cowbar provides shelter for numerous small fishing vessels

(Right) The famous 199 steps provide a breathtaking panorama - in more than one way!

(Below) The ancient St. Mary's Church closely associated with the famous Dracula Legend

(Above) The enormous whalebone arch on Whitby's West Cliff provides a splendid vantage point

(Below) Part of Whitby's busy fishing and recreational harbour

(Below) The sandy beach and rugged headland of Whitby's East Cliff

Introduction to Places to Visit & Things to Do

It is difficult to imagine being able to cover this vast area satisfactorily in just one tour, and visitors may feel compelled to return to sample again the delights of the North York Moors. However, there are a few places which should be on anybody's 'must-see' selection list.

Over the years, the **North York Moors Railway** and the **Esk Valley Railway** have had a huge impact on the area. The North York Moors Railway, for example, is still the only way you can reach some parts of **Newtondale.** It is even possible to take a meal as you travel the length of its eighteen miles and back again, at a gentle twenty-five miles an hour (and less on gradients!) that will allow you to take in the scenery. Children will enjoy this return to the age of steam, and the walks that spread out from each of the stations along the way on both lines allow considerable latitude for exploration.

The historic North York Moors Railway

When you visit the North York Moors Railway, why not take in **Pickering,** which is the terminus of the line? It is a fine market town, with **a ruined castle,** and **a fascinating ancient church** with excellent C15th murals of Thomas à Becket and St George and the dragon, among others.

However, if castles are of particular interest to you then as well as **Pickering Castle** there are several others well worth a visit. **Helmsley Castle in Duncombe Park** is a vast and impressive ruin dating back to the C12th. Another option would be to visit the massive ruins of **Scarborough Castle,** shelled by the German High Seas Fleet in the First World War, and then take the opportunity to wander round the lovely gardens that make Scarborough so special.

The spectacular ruins of **Rievaulx Abbey** with soaring arches, presents a setting of peace, serenity, and a marvellous freedom from the tumult of the world.

It may be, however, that you are caught in the rain, and need to be inside, in which case there is every reason to visit the **Captain Cook Birthplace Museum,** set in the beautifully landscaped grounds of Stewart Park, Marton, which records the exciting days when the extent of the known world and its riches leapt under the exploring eye of the great man himself. Displays illustrate the natural history of Australia, new Zealand, Canada and the South Seas, together with the weapons of their peoples, and make it easy to understand the huge impact these would have made upon the sailors who first saw them.

Further inland is an outstanding museum with exhibits recording life much closer to home than the Cook Museum. **The Ryedale Folk Museum** at **Hutton-le-Hole** won no less than three major awards in 1995. It spreads over 1 hectare (2.5 acres), and three of its finest exhibits are buildings: these thatched cruck-framed houses were re-erected on this site after facing demolition, and now house collections that give a fascinating insight into the past life of this unique corner of Yorkshire. The museum has both temporary and permanent exhibitions... and, of course, the annual world championship of the game called Merrills (Nine Man's Morris).

Most of the villages in the area are worth a visit too, but particularly **Goathland** and **Lealholm,** which are both outstandingly pretty. Alternatively you could turn your nose seawards and visit **Staithes, Whitby** or **Robin Hood's Bay** for the taste of smuggling, fishing, and an old isolation from the world.

For those who feel nothing for ruins, trains, or museums, there are two further options. There is a huge variety of **outdoor activities** available in the area - it is, for example, very good for fishing. However, the last option is perhaps the best choice of all on this page: to walk into the high moorlands with a stout pair of boots on your feet and a map in your hand, and in this way to discover nature's beauty, and the purpose for which the North York Moors seem expressly to have been designed.

Outdoor Activities

The North Yorkshire Moors and Coast provide a wide selection of outdoor leisure activities for you to enjoy, **whether participant or spectator.** You must, however, be aware of several important facts. First, nearly all the land is under private ownership and permission must first be granted before access obtained; secondly, membership of some clubs is essential if you are to utilize their facilities; and finally, **please remain aware of the dangers** of climate, particularly if you are to venture onto the open expanses of moor, forest or sea. The weather can change very rapidly, so please take no chances and be fully prepared and equipped. The National Park produces a leaflet 'Moorland Safety', which is well worth close study. Remember, the lives of you and your family and friends are at risk; for example sudden mists and icy temperatures at altitude can be dangerous even in summer. Those returning onto the North Sea should be fully experienced and take regular advice on weather and sea conditions to ensure their safety.

Now, well-warned to be fully knowledgeable of the hazards, consider the **exciting range of outdoor activities** the countryside and coast of this area offer: **walking, climbing, orienteering, shooting, gliding, sailing, swimming, fishing, water-skiing, windsurfing** and **golf.** To obtain a full list of outdoor activities and details about them we recommend that you contact the Tourist Information Centres in the area.

One of the best ways to view this beautiful region is from the air. **Hang gliding** is popular at Sutton Bank, which is also the home of **the Yorkshire Gliding Club,** but another form of leaving the ground is **microlight flying** for which trial lessons can be arranged. And while the adults get airborne, children can get in on the act too, with **kite flying.**

However, the most popular way of enjoying this magnificent region is with your feet firmly on the ground. **Walking** is very popular, with public rights of way being well marked and published walks being widely available, including some from the National Park Centres that also produce their own walks leaflets and books. Furthermore, should you wish to participate in a fully organised walk, then both the **Moors Centre** and **Sutton Bank Visitor Centre** hold regular **Sunday walks** throughout the summer for those who like a friendly crowd on their rambles.

The rivers of the area provide several very popular activities, not least **fishing.** Obviously there is great participation in **sea fishing** along the long coastline of the area, but the rivers have their own important part to play in this sport. The beautiful River Esk, from which Whitby's drinking water is drawn, is the only established north-eastern migratory **salmon** river and, for much of the year, the fishermen live on the banks and you can join them if you purchase a license. It is even possible to hire tackle if you came here without.

As for those who prefer a form of pastime 'on the river', there are **pleasure boats** and even **canoes** to tour the rivers in. Of course, this is an ideal way for **birdwatchers** to enjoy the rich variety of **birdlife** along the sheltered unpolluted waters. There are teal, the smallest breed of duck, and their larger cousins, the mallards and muscovies. If you are very lucky, you may also catch sight of the vivid flash of colour which is a passing kingfisher; and there may also be moorhens and cormorants in abundance. At evening, a heron may even float magically in to fish for their supper on the weirs. When the river is in flood and the water running fast over the weir, they may even take salmon and eels as you watch.

For those lovers of nature the rich variety of habitats along the **coast,** in the dales, on the moors and in the **forest** support a tremendous range of flora and fauna. However, one rather unique location that many may wish to visit is **the Honey Farm** at East Ayton which is a working honey farm, with unrivalled opportunities to study the insects who make your tasty pot of honey possible.

Perhaps a less tiring method of exploration and enjoyment would be **on horseback.** It is always tempting to some to take advantage of the qualified **riding centres** in the area that offer a different viewpoint and perspective on the landscape.

There are so many activities available in and around the area that it is impossible to mention them all here - but they include the opportunity to jump off a cliff on an **abseil** rope, go **white water rafting, orienteering,** or to **cycle** round the National Park on any one of three 'Pedal and Puff' routes that link with stations on the North Yorkshire Moors Railway. Come to think of it perhaps the most comfortable way to enjoy the great outdoors is **by train** on such as the Esk Valley and North York Moors Railways. or by car on the many quiet country lanes that serve this historic and beautiful region. The choice is all yours!

The North York Moors Railway

IF YOU WISH TO VISIT NEWTONDALE, you have no option but to take the train! No road travels the length of this deeply wooded dale, so this is your cue to take a trip into nostalgia on the North Yorkshire Moors Railway.

THE NORTH YORKSHIRE MOORS RAILWAY enjoys a well-documented and intriguing history. During the early C19th, Whitby businessmen were becoming **increasingly concerned about the isolation of the town,** which had for years relied upon the North Sea as its principal means of communication. In order to link the town with its hinterland, it was proposed to construct a canal through Newtondale to Pickering. However, the opening of the now-famous Stockton to Darlington Railway in 1825 influenced the parties involved to consider a railway instead of a canal, and **George Stephenson** was brought in to engineer the line.

Considering that the labour on the line was all man-powered, **the speed of the line's construction was remarkable.** As level as possible a track was hewn through the rock by hand, the stone was barrowed away, and a great series of bridges was also built - and then there was still the track itself to lay, along 24 miles of a route so serpentine that many jokes were made about it. **Starting at Whitby, the line pushed up the Esk valley to Grosmont,** where a **tunnel was dug** through the hillside to gain access to the valley of the Murk Esk.

SOUTH FROM HERE, AT BECK HOLE, a 1,400 metre incline with a gradient of 1 in 15 was constructed, up which **carriages were hauled by rope.** The line continued to the south, and after crossing Fen Bog, entered the glacial gorge of Newtondale to continue on to Pickering. This railway was **originally a simple coach drawn along the rails by horses.** When the railway was officially opened in 1836, there was a great and, it seems, noisy celebration. Brass bands played, church bells were rung and cannon were fired - and on the inaugural run, 'Lady Hilda', one of the coaches, came off the rails three times!

IN 1845, THE 'RAILWAY KING', George **Hudson,** bought the line and, in order to link it with his expanding railway network and also with a view to extending his property interests in Whitby, he spent a great deal of money on improvements. These included **the introduction of steam** to the line and the construction of a deviation line (to cut out the old incline) which opened in 1865 and is the route used by the present railway. The original route makes a pleasant walk between Goathland and Grosmont. **The postwar years were sad ones** for the railways, many of which fell into decline and were closed; and this area was no exception, although the Pickering to Whitby line was always used for regular excursion trains. When British Rail finally closed the line between Grosmont and Pickering in 1965, there were loudly-voiced protests from many people who had grown to love this remarkable line, and within two years the **North Yorkshire Moors Historical Railway Trust** had been formed. With a tremendous amount of effort and enthusiasm, they first managed to re-open the line between Grosmont and Goathland, and later, on the 1st of May 1973, the complete line between Grosmont and Pickering was re-opened for passenger traffic by **the Duchess of Kent.**

Since then, it has proved to be a most popular and, by now, profitable attraction. The secret is that 'the route is one of surpassing beauty', as the York Courant of the 2nd of June 1836 said when the line was opened. That remains equally true today. Its very inaccessibility has left the post-glacial gorge of Newtondale unspoilt and not a little **awe-inspiring and mysterious.** The geology of this deep gorge is, of course, fascinating, and the North Yorkshire Moors Railway booklet, entitled 'Guideline', has a very useful page on this geological 'corridor' between Grosmont and Pickering, as well as on the Cleveland Dyke, the great outcropping whinstone ridge from which so much roadstone has been quarried.

This same booklet gives an extremely clear route map, with frequent and helpful notes on the sights to be seen from the train and the attractions that can be visited from the various halts along its route. It also provides information on **the Historical Railway Trail** that starts from Goathland, where there are lovely woodlands walks with a series of waterfalls or at the **Newtondale Halt,** where waymarked paths lead to wild moorland vantage points, giving breathtaking views of the surrounding countryside.

Finally, the two places at the ends of the line are equally interesting: **Pickering** with its fine ruined castle, ancient church and the very interesting **Beck Isle Museum of Rural Life;** and **Grosmont,** where a specially constructed viewing gallery gives excellent views of all the line's engines, while the Trust's members are working on them. All of this makes a trip on this historic railway **an experience to treasure.**

The Esk Valley Line

RAIL ENTHUSIASTS visiting this part of Yorkshire will find many delights in store, because the area is fortunate enough to possess two of the most attractive railway lines in the country.

One of these is the **Esk Valley Line,** running west to east from **Cleveland to Whitby,** and widely regarded as one of the most scenically appealing in the whole of the British railway network.That network used to be much more extensive than it is today.

THE ESK VALLEY LINE begins at **Middlesbrough,** and the line to Middlesbrough was one of the first to be added to the famous Stockton and Darlington Railway, in 1830. An extension onwards, from Middlesbrough to **Nunthorpe,** was not opened until 1854, however, and this turned out to be the first stage in creating a rail link right along the Esk Valley. The final stretch to **Grosmont** was completed in 1868, and this provided a connecting point with **the Pickering to Whitby railway,** already quite a 'veteran' line, having been opened in 1836. It is that line which is now **the North Yorkshire Moors Railway.**

The Esk Valley Line, as we use it today, is actually made up from stretches 'borrowed' from no less than four early C19th railways, all **constructed during the boom years** of ironstone mining. The boom lasted some forty years, from around 1860-1900, and during this period vast quantities of ironstone had to be transported to the blast furnaces of Middlesbrough; thus grew up **a complex network of small mineral railways,** all linking back to the Esk Valley. But by about 1930 almost all these minor lines had closed down. Now, only the Esk Valley Railway remains, passing through some of the most beautiful scenery in the North York Moors

The line **starts** from Middlesbrough, a lively town with an interesting industrial heritage. One notable landmark is the famous **Transporter Bridge.** Middlesbrough has good facilities for shopping, entertainment and leisure pursuits, along with the **Dorman Museum** of local history, several galleries displaying both art and craft, and the **Newham Grange Leisure Farm. Marton** and **Great Ayton** are important stops along the next section, before the line enters **Upper Eskdale** where the River Esk, Yorkshire's

only salmon river, meanders across the wide, flat floor of the valley. In **Lower Eskdale,** river and rail compete for position in the narrow, steep gorges, where the railway bridges cross the Esk 16 times in only 11 miles .

THE STATIONS ALONG THE WAY offer access to the North York Moors countryside in all its different moods. For instance, one of the earlier stops is at **Castleton Moor,** where geologists can seek out the source of the River Esk as it emerges from the volcanic basalt of the exposed rocks. Here you will be met by the bracing wind and wild, upland scenery. Not much further on, however, you will find instead snug villages such as **Lealholm,** comfortably settled in the lush green of the valley floor. Only a little further on, the scene changes again, to the sea breezes and the cries of the gulls as they wheel over the fishing boats at **Whitby.** Here are all the ingredients of an old-fashioned seaside holiday.

At all these stopping places, the stations are equipped with **helpful information boards,** welcoming visitors to the local attractions, such as the **Moors Centre at Danby,** where all nature lovers will be enthralled by the excellent wildlife displays, or the interesting collection of old locomotives and rolling stock maintained at Grosmont. Another name for the line might almost be the **Captain Cook Line,** for its stops include not only **Marton** (where he was born) but also **Great Ayton** (where he grew up) and **Whitby** (where he learnt his seamanship). All three locations have fascinating museums which, between them, tell the story of Cook's life in intimate detail.

In addition to places to visit, **routes for walking** are indicated at each stop along the line, and nearly every village can offer its own pub too, serving traditional ales and bar meals, sometimes even in the former station buildings! **Picnics** are made easy and convenient as well, with tables and benches provided in pleasant surroundings near many stations.

If you buy a **Ranger ticket,** you can make use of as many of the local trains as you wish in a day, getting off at any stop you choose and continuing on a later train. Day trips further afield are no problem either. Indeed, the advantage of a rail journey to Durham or York is that it liberates you from all the problems of driving in city traffic and having to find somewhere to park your car. All in all, **if you want to visit Eskdale, you can not do better than take a train** on this wholly delightful line. You will travel in comfort, enjoying the scenery in a way not really possible from a car, and at the end of the day, you really will have savoured a trip to remember.

Castles of the Area

Castles were introduced by the Normans in order to quell the rebellious North after the conquest. Repeated Scottish raids and frequent quarrels among the Norman lords also contributed to the importance of the castles in the area. The form of the castle roughly remained the same: a wall surrounded the wide expanse of the 'bailey', in the centre of which was a 'motte' (or earth mound) surmounted by another wall. The motte was the last line of defence, and was transformed in the mid-C12th when it was built of stone, and became a 'keep'.

Over the next 300 years, towers, curtain walls, bridges and portcullises were added to the basic design. However, when peace eventually settled over the region, many castles fell into disrepair, and were plundered as 'quarries' by local builders. Except during the Civil War in the C17th, the castles never returned to their original purpose, but became either homes or ruins.

It is advisable to check at local Tourist Information Centres for the opening days and times of all the properties listed, as not many are open daily and several only open on one or two days a week.

Within the area covered by this guide, there are nearly thirty castle sites, most of them no more than mounds with grassed-over walls and ditches.

Less substantial remains than those listed below are found at Castleton, where the C11th motte survives, and at Danby, a palace-cum-fortress built in the C14th by the Latimer family. This castle was for a time the home of Catherine Parr, who was married to the third Lord Neville before she became the wife of Henry VIII. It is privately owned and not usually open to the public. On the western fringe of the moors, the small but imposing C14th gatehouse of Whorlton Castle displays the arms of the Meynell family, and other sites may be found at Ayton, Brompton, Cropton, Kildale, Kirkbymoorside and Mulgrave.

GILLING CASTLE, Helmsley. It is chiefly the garden and grounds which will attract visitors. The castle is a pot pourri of architectural styles centred on a basic Norman keep. As the Castle is used as a prep school for Ampleforth College, only the Entrance Hall and the stunning late C16th Great Chamber (termtime only) are open to visitors, but these justify a visit. Meanwhile, the gardens, part formal, part landscaped, offer delightful walks.

HELMSLEY CASTLE (EH) These gaunt remains, set in Duncombe Park, are most extensive and impressive. The oldest surviving parts date from the late C12th, and are ascribed to the Lord of Helmsley, Robert de Roos. Later owners added the Barbican and Chapel and the Great Hall and Buttery. Inside, its size, style and grandeur are soon experienced. It has been of relatively little historical importance. It was owned by the de Roos family until 1508, when it was sold to Sir Charles Duncombe, to whom the present Earl of Feversham is related. Its most important moment came in the Civil War when it was besieged in 1644 by Sir Thomas Fairfax and 1000 troops. After three months it surrendered under Colonel Crossland and the castle structure was rendered unusable.

PICKERING CASTLE (EH), Its compactness provides much of its attraction, enabling one to appreciate the various stages of castle development. Its dominant feature is the mighty earthen motte, dating from the time of William the Conqueror. The early wooden keep was replaced by the present stone one in the C12th. After Robert the Bruce invaded from Scotland in 1322, the castle was strengthened with outer walls and towers. Edward II visited in 1323 and Richard II was held prisoner here, before being moved to Pontefract, where he was killed. For the greater part of its existence, it was used as a residence for royalty while hunting in the Royal Forest of Pickering nearby.

SCARBOROUGH CASTLE (EH) In a most impressive setting, its extensive remains stand on the lofty Castle Headland overlooking the town of Scarborough and the North Sea. The site had been used as a signal station by the Romans about 800 years before the Norman castle's construction in 1158. In the C12th it was besieged by Henry II; in the C13th, King John spent the then astronomical sum of £2000 on defensive improvements; in the C14th it was granted by Edward II to his favourite, Piers Gaveston; and in the C17th, as the last Royalist outpost on the East Coast, it was besieged by Cromwell himself, surrendering in 1645. From 1665-6 George Fox, founder of the Quaker Movement, was imprisoned here, and its last appearance in the pages of history came in 1914 when it was badly damaged by German warships. Today it is of a more peaceful nature, and from its windswept ruins can be enjoyed fine panoramic views.

Halls & Gardens of the Area

There are many attractive and interesting historic buildings and gardens in this region, which is a tribute to the wealth and power of the aristocrats and merchants of the area over the centuries... but also to their good taste!

Relatively few are open to the public, and once again, it is worth ringing in advance to check opening times, but those that are open more than compensate for the lack of the others. In many of these mansions, the appeal of a visit lies in the fascinating history of the previous owners - warriors, statesmen and writers - as much as the beauty of the building themselves.

DUNCOMBE PARK, Helmsley. This imposing mansion was designed by William Wakefield of Easingwold, a pupil of Vanbrugh - the master was working on Castle Howard at the same time. Two successive fires in the late C19th destroyed much of the house and it was later rebuilt, though not precisely to the original plans. After many years as a girls' preparatory school, it has recently returned to use as the home of the Feversham family and was opened to the public for the first time in 1990. The house is set in outstandingly beautiful formal gardens, containing two C18th temples and a magnificent grass terrace overlooking the ruins of Rievaulx Abbey. This is separated from the nearby Rievaulx Terraces by a valley which Thomas Duncombe, who built Duncombe Park in 1713, had planned to bridge with a massive viaduct - a scheme so enormous as to seem quite fantastic today.

EBBERSTON HALL, near Scarborough. This is a very small Palladian villa built in 1718 to designs by Colen Campbell. Internally, it has many beautiful and decorative features both in plaster and in wood, reminiscent of Castle Howard. It is pleasing to be able to report that the owners, who welcome visitors in person, are in the process of restoring the once celebrated water gardens, which include a lengthy cascade and a 350 metres canal. Ornamental fowl, deer and Jacob sheep can be seen in the grounds.

HOVINGHAM HALL, York. Despite its address, this fine Palladian house actually lies between Malton and Helmsley. It was designed by Thomas Worsley in the mid-C18th and his family (of whom the present Duchess of Kent is the best known member) have lived there ever since. The house contains fine furniture, ornaments and family portraits. The grounds contain an unusually-designed riding school and a private cricket ground. Please note that this property is open to parties of over fifteen, by written appointment only. The surrounding village of Hovingham is worth visiting anyway, however, as it contains several interesting buildings, among them a church which is Anglo-Saxon in origin, and a pleasant Georgian inn named the Worsley Arms.

NEWBURGH PRIORY, Coxwold. This is detailed here, rather than under 'Abbeys' because, although it has its origins as a C12th religious foundation, it has been the private home of a single family since 1538. An attic room is thought to contain, surprisingly, the mortal remains of Oliver Cromwell, whose third daughter, Mary, was married to a former owner of Newburgh Priory, Viscount Fauconberg. The wild water garden, containing many rare plants, some alpines and fine rhododendrons, is captivatingly beautiful. Afternoon teas are available.

NUNNINGTON HALL (NT), near Helmsley. A charming and characterful C16th manor house, which was a private home until recently, when it was restored by the National Trust. It has a very fine staircase and many intimate panelled and tapestry-hung rooms, typical of the period. The attic contains a collection of one-eighth life-size miniature rooms which will delight children. Visitors can also enjoy afternoon tea in the Dining Room or a picnic in the riverside garden.

ORMESBY HALL (NT), Middlesbrough. Exquisite plasterwork adorns this C18th house, which replaced a Jacobean mansion on the same site. Also C18th is the excellent Stable Block, probably by Carr of York. The garden is attractive and there is a tea-room and shop.

OSGODBY HALL, near Thirsk. This is a small, private Jacobean Hall, very much a home and one around which the owners show visitors in person. It boasts a particularly fine C17th forecourt and staircase. Teas are available by arrangement.

RIEVAULX TERRACE (NT), Helmsley. Nothing could provide a finer example of C18th landscape design, nor a better demonstration of the incredible scale on which landscaping projects were undertaken. It was created in 1758 by Thomas Duncombe, to echo the similar terrace at Duncombe Park and to provide long, level walks with magnificent views over Ryedale. At each end of the half-mile-long terrace is a classical temple, that to the north being decorated by the Italian artist

Burnici and executed by him, Sistine Chapel style, over a period of seven years! It is furnished as a dining room and was used for family picnics. The other temple, to the southern end of the Terrace, is a Doric or Tuscan-style rotunda, less elaborately decorated but with a fine domed and coffered ceiling. Wheelchairs are provided for disabled visitors.

The grandeur of Rievaulx Temples

SALTBURN and **SCARBOROUGH**, both contain historically interesting municipal gardens, designed for public enjoyment. Scarborough's gardens are particularly attractive and varied and are a prominent feature of this once spa town. In both towns, the gardens are maintained with pride.

SHANDY HALL, Coxwold. This was, from 1760 until his death in 1768, the home of Coxwold's eccentric local parson, Laurence Sterne. The liberal tone of his books, such as 'Tristram Shandy' and 'A Sentimental Journey' - as well as his own philanderings - made him a figure of some notoriety! The house, though still lived in, is owned by the Laurence Sterne Trust. It is small and intimate, and contains many interesting mementoes of its former owner. Built as a timber-framed house in the C15th, it was added to in the C17th and Sterne himself made some rather odd improvements in the C18th. Its setting, in well-maintained traditional cottage gardens, adds to its attraction. Another fine Coxwold building is the Fauconberg Arms, an appealing old inn dating from the C17th. Other buildings of the same period include the old Manor House, named Colville Hall, and the Old Hall, which used to be a grammar school. The perpendicular church is C15th in origin. Coxwold has much to offer of architectural distinction. Its unspoilt charm makes it a 'must' for all lovers of traditional English villages.

SION HILL HALL, Kirby Wiske, near Thirsk. This is an attractive country house in neo-Georgian style, where visitors can enjoy fine furniture, pictures and an especially impressive collection of porcelain.

SIR WILLIAM TURNER'S HOSPITAL, Kirkleatham. These beautiful almshouses, probably the finest in Britain, form the centrepiece of a village of some architectural distinction. The hospital was founded in 1668 by Sir William Turner, a noted local philanthropist knighted by Charles II, partly in gratitude for his munificent donations to the royal revenues. The building is in two wings either side of a chapel - and it is this chapel that is the real jewel, for it was designed in the workshop of one of Sir William's friends, none other than Sir Christopher Wren. The two wings offered accommodation to twenty destitute men and women, and a school was available to local children, making the whole a remarkable charitable concept for so early a date. Turner himself is buried in a massive, ornate mausoleum in St Cuthbert's Church, which is not far away.

Finally, a few attractions which are just outside the area covered by this guide

CASTLE HOWARD, near Malton. Known to television viewers as Brideshead, after the dramatisation of Evelyn Waugh's 'Brideshead Revisited', this great house was designed by Sir John Vanbrugh, perhaps the C18th's most imaginative architect. Set amidst beautiful and colourful landscaped gardens, this family home is open to the public. There is much to see, for, as well as the grandeur of its architecture and furnishings, including Chippendale, Sheraton and Adam, there is an amazing collection of paintings by Rubens, Gainsborough, Holbein, Reynolds and others. In the coach-houses, there is the largest collection of privately-owned period costumes in Britain.

SHERIFF HUTTON PARK, north of York. James I's former hunting lodge is open to the public more than before, and its delightful grounds are a major attraction.

SUTTON PARK, near Easingwold, on the York to Helmsley road. This house was built in 1730, a few years after Castle Howard, and contains exquisite furnishings, on a less intimidating scale. The gardens are justifiably famous, especially noted for the woodland walks in spring through carpets of daffodils.

Abbeys of the Area

Within the area there are over twenty sites of medieval religious houses, though only a few remain in any substantial form. Monastic settlements were first established in this country as early as AD 596 and in the north of England the two branches of Christianity, the Celtic and the Roman, were both represented. The great growth of major religious houses in the area did not take place until after the Norman Conquest in the C11th, however, when it became common practice for Norman barons, hoping to find favour with God as well as respect from their peers, to grant areas of land to groups of monks on which to found a settlement. With the help of armies of lay brothers, these monks then developed such interests as sheep farming, salt pans, iron foundries and fisheries to produce the income with which to extend and improve their churches. Their very prosperity, however, made the Dissolution of the Monasteries under Henry VIII in 1538 almost inevitable, as they were now perceived to have disproportionate wealth and influence.

The impressive remains of Byland Abbey

The better known settlements in this area had a purely religious function, but others were devoted to attending the sick or protecting pilgrims. Today, their remains are found in beautiful and peaceful surroundings but, when founded so many centuries ago, they were established in a true wilderness, such as the remote valley of Ryedale or the wet marshlands of Byland. Even in their ruined state, they provide a window on a whole field of history that played a crucial part in the development of our area.

AMPLEFORTH By far the last to have been built, dating from 1802 when Benedictine monks (the same order who had founded Westminster Abbey) brought the religious community life back to North Yorkshire. Their school has become the leading Roman Catholic independent school in the country and was for many years home to His Eminence Cardinal Basil Hume, first as a student and later as abbot.

BYLAND ABBEY (EH) The Savigniac monks who founded Byland came originally from Furness Abbey in the Lake District. After an abortive attempt in 1134 to establish Calder Abbey in Cumberland (later achieved), they returned to Furness Abbey in 1138 and received new orders to travel to York and seek the patronage of Archbishop Thurstan. On the way, they came to Thirsk, where they met Lady Gundreda and her son Roger de Mowbray and were persuaded to settle locally. Sites at Hood below Sutton Bank, Old Byland north of Rievaulx, and Stocking, were all tried before they finally fixed on the present location in 1177. The period at Stocking saw the order of Savigny absorbed into the Cistercian order. The ruins of this 'much travelled' abbey are quite impressive, particularly the west window. Another famous feature is the floor, geometrically patterned with yellow and green glazed tiles, now rather worn and incomplete but still giving an impression of its former glory. Sheltering here after the Battle of Byland in 1322, Edward II was nearly taken captive by Robert the Bruce.

GUISBOROUGH PRIORY This impressive ruin on the edge of the moors was an Augustinian house founded in 1119 by Robert de Brus.

KIRKHAM PRIORY (EH) Another C12th Augustinian house. Founded on land granted by Walter L'Espec in memory of his son killed in a hunting accident. Its ruins are fragmentary, but the peaceful location is attractive and a good display of late C13th heraldry is seen at the gatehouse.

LASTINGHAM The real birthplace of Christianity in the area; the C7th King Ethelwald asked St Cedd of Lindisfarne to found a monastery here. The original building survived some 200 years but was destroyed by Danish invaders around AD 870. In 1078, Stephen, a Benedictine monk from Whitby, re-established a community here but they were harassed into departing for York. What remains is one of the finest Norman crypts in England, a virtual church in itself.

MOUNT GRACE PRIORY (NT, EH) Founded in 1398 and located near Osmotherley, it is the only Carthusian house in the area and the best preserved of the nine in the country. Carthusians lived in virtual silence and isolation, rarely seeing each other except for one communal meal a week. Each monk had his own house or cell, together with a small garden, and these are ranged around sizeable cloisters. Again, the setting is beautiful and a great sense of peace is all-pervading. The original Priory Guest House, converted into a Jacobean Manor House by Thomas Lascelles in 1654, is now a TIC, exhibition centre and souvenir shop.

NEWBURGH PRIORY (See 'Halls and Gardens').

OLD MALTON boasts some remains of a Gilbertine priory, founded between 1147 and 1154, and the only English representative of the order founded by Gilbert of Sempringham in 1131. Though about half these foundations were dual, with monks in one house and nuns in another, St Mary's Priory at Malton was for men only.

RIEVAULX ABBEY (EH) One of the most celebrated - and perhaps the most beautiful - in the country. It was founded in 1132 by thirteen Cistercian monks from Clairvaux in France, also on land granted by Walter l'Espec (see 'Kirkham Priory'). By 1147, when the abbot was Aeldred (later canonised) it had 140 monks and 500 lay brothers. The construction of the church and other buildings progressed at a rapid pace, using stone transported by a purpose-built canal. Sizeable fish ponds were also constructed and the monks' sheep farming and mining interests were extensive, but, by the late C13th, the monastery was heavily in debt as a result of considerable repairs and extensions. At the Dissolution in 1538, much was destroyed, in particular the monks' living quarters, to prevent their return. But the main church, with its three tiers of soaring arches, remains surprisingly complete and it takes only a small leap of the imagination to see it in its former glory. One service a year, an early communion, takes place in the ruins and is a uniquely moving occasion. Rievaulx's own greatest Abbot, St Aeldred, summarised the quality of the place when he said, 'Everywhere peace, everywhere serenity, and a marvellous freedom from the tumult of the world'.

ROSEDALE ABBEY A tiny priory founded in 1138, housing only ten nuns of the Cistercian order. The present church has been built on its site, but of the original building the name is almost all that remains.

The beautiful setting of St. Gregory's Minster

ST GREGORY'S MINSTER A mile west of Kirkbymoorside. Though never the focus of a large religious community, it is sufficiently exceptional to merit a mention. Visitors will be disappointed if they expect a large building but, hopefully, its style, history and setting will be compensation. The origins of this church go back at least to the C8th. Its most famous feature is the pre-Conquest sundial set into the wall over the entrance. Dating from between 1055 and 1064, it is the best example of its kind in the country.

WHITBY ABBEY (EH) Its impressive ruins have an imposing position on the cliff-top overlooking the town. It was the earliest major foundation in the area. In AD 657, King Oswy founded the Abbey as a thanks-offering to God for his victory over King Penda, and installed his daughter, Hilda, as the first Abbess. They presided together over the Synod of Whitby in AD 664, and when Hilda died in AD 680, she was buried in the Abbey, later being recognised as a saint. It was Hilda who recognised and fostered the remarkable talent of the poor cowherd, Caedmon, now acclaimed as the creator of religious verse in English. The ghost of St Hilda is said to appear at one of the Abbey windows - you only have to wait long enough and you will see her! The fact that the Abbey was largely destroyed in AD 867, during Viking raids, and restored in 1078 in the Benedictine Order, rather than that of Iona, does not seem to matter.

Museums & Galleries of the Area

Not all Museums are open on a daily basis, even in season, and some charge (usually modest) admission fees. You should make further enquiries at local Tourist Information Centres.

AMPLEFORTH MINIATURE STEAM RAILWAY, Old Station, Ampleforth. This friendly little railway opened in 1989 and offers a perfect nostalgic afternoon out. Nearby is Thorpe Hall Farm's collection of old farming machinery.

ART GALLERY, The Crescent, Scarborough. Housed in an attractive C19th villa, this gallery displays English paintings of local interest and mounts frequent special exhibitions.

BECK ISLE MUSEUM OF RURAL LIFE , Pickering. This fine little museum depicts life in the Victorian era; each room follows a theme, such as an olde worlde inn, cobbler's shop, children's room, front parlour, printer's shop and photography room. Outbuildings house farm implements and machinery.

CAPTAIN COOK BIRTHPLACE MUSEUM, Stewart Park, Marton. Set in beautiful parkland, this award-winning museum has displays rich in the atmosphere of Cook's early life, and examples of tools, weapons and cultures that he found on his travels

CAPTAIN COOK MEMORIAL MUSEUM, Grape Lane, Whitby. This elegant town house was the home of Cook's employer, ship-owner John Walker. It is furnished according to the family's own inventory and additional displays include original manuscripts, watercolours and drawings. Visitors can also see the attic where, according to tradition, Cook and the other 'servants' and apprentices were lodged.

CAPTAIN COOK SCHOOLROOM MUSEUM, Great Ayton. This fascinating little museum houses personal relics of the Cook family and an interesting collection of early maps, pictures and photographs.

DALBY VISITOR CENTRE, Low Dalby. This excellent informative centre is found in the magnificent surroundings of the coniferous Dalby Forest. It outlines the objectives of the Forestry Commission, who operate the Centre. The displays on wildlife are a great attraction.

THE DRACULA EXPERIENCE, 9 Marine Parade, Whitby. This ingenious, spine-chilling exhibit has won an English Tourist Board award.

EDEN CAMP MODERN HISTORY THEME MUSEUM, Malton. This well organised museum provides an insight into the hardships of everyday civilian life that went on while the second world war was being fought and won.

EDEN FARM INSIGHT, Old Malton. This working farm gives an exceptional opportunity to learn about crop-farming (though there are plenty of animals too) past and present.

THE EXHIBITION CENTRE, Goathland. A relatively recent attraction depicting the history and heritage of Goathland and the surrounding area - plus a 'Heartbeat' Exhibition

THE HONEY FARM, East Ayton, Scarborough. There is so much more than honey to the honey farm: a pottery, farm animals and craft and gift shops all augment the central attraction: the bees themselves. You'll never be this close to a bee again without getting stung.

KIRKLEATHAM OWL CENTRE, Redcar. This is one of the largest bird of prey centres in the north of England, with flying displays from 12 noon each day, weather permitting.

LIGHTHOUSE AND FISHERIES MUSEUM, Vincent Pier, Scarborough. This interesting little museum is seen, level by level, as you climb to the top of the small lighthouse itself. The history of lighthouses and of the local fishing community is told in atmospheric surroundings.

MALTON MUSEUM, Market Place, Malton. Set in the C18th Town Hall, this museum has one of the most important archaeological collections of the area. The Roman remains connected with the nearby Roman town of Derventio are of especial interest. The first floor of the building has been refurbished to provide a gallery where a variety of exhibitions are staged.

THE MOORS CENTRE, Danby. See feature on 'The North York Moors National Park'.

MUSIC IN MINIATURE EXHIBITION, Robin Hood's Bay, Whitby. This contains fifty one-twelfth dioramic scale models, with a theme of music from BC to the present day.

PANNETT ART GALLERY, Pannett Park, Whitby. A good collection of English watercolours and oils by artists past and present, with Turner probably the most famous name among several fine artists represented.

PICKERING MODEL RAILWAY EXHIBITION, 7 Park Street, Pickering. Four layouts, including one for children, of scenic model railways.

PLANETARIUM, Alexandra Gardens, Scarborough. This is apparently the first planetarium to be situated in a seaside resort, and here it is found in most appealing surroundings. It features a 'night sky' around which visitors are skilfully guided.

ROTUNDA MUSEUM, Vernon Road, Scarborough. Built in 1829 and named after its shape, it was originally designed by William Smith, the 'Father of English Geology', to house his local geological collection. Today, a frieze round the inside of the domed roof depicts a geological section along the Yorkshire Coast, but the displays are now largely devoted to aspects of regional archaeology. Indeed, it is often referred to as the Archaeological Museum. The two wings were added in 1960, some time after Smith's death in 1839.

RYEDALE FOLK MUSEUM, Hutton-le-Hole. Opened in 1964 to celebrate the daily lives of the people of Ryedale from prehistoric to recent times, a part of history that would otherwise have been lost. There are reconstructed cruck-framed houses, and fascinating exhibitions on all aspects of craft and life of the locality.

SAINT MARY'S MUSEUM OF CHURCH ART, Levisham. Run by the Society for the Promotion of the Preservation of English Parish Churches, this unique museum exhibits the history of church art and architecture over the centuries - and is itself housed in a beautiful example of both: the lovely Church of St Mary, which is Anglo-Saxon in origin.

A model of the Endeavour suspended in Middlesbrough's Cleveland Centre

SION HILL HALL AND BIRDS OF PREY CENTRE, Sion Hill Hall, Kirby Wiske, Thirsk. The beautiful surroundings of this Edwardian Hall frame an extensive collection of antique furniture, porcelein, and pictures, while the walled garden houses the Birds of Prey and Conservation Centre: an excellent way to combine two sorts of visit in one day.

SPOUT HOUSE, Bilsdale. This is an original cruck-framed house, now carefully restored to show the interesting features of this traditional local style of architecture.

THE SUTCLIFFE GALLERY, Flowergate, Whitby. Born in Leeds in 1853, Frank Meadow Sutcliffe came to Whitby with his family in 1871. He was already experimenting with photography, and eventually established his studio here. Keeping his memory alive has been a personal crusade for Bill Eglon Shaw who, now with the help of his son, runs this excellent gallery. Outstanding prints from Sutcliffe's original negatives are sold - a rare chance to obtain an example of the work of a true master of the photographic art.

THIRSK BIRD MUSEUM, 87b Market Place, Thirsk. A beautifully presented collection of stuffed birds, full of information and interest.

THREE MARINERS' INN, Scarborough. This one-time inn, with its secret passages and smuggling connections, is now an intriguing little museum, privately run and making the most of this romantic old building.

TOCKETTS WATERMILL, Guisborough. The last survivor of the watermills of Cleveland, saved to continue work that it has done for the last six centuries. Here are four storeys full of the moving shadows of the water-wheel, the light dust of fresh-milled flour, and the vibration of the machinery through the floorboards.

TOM LEONARD MINING MUSEUM, Skinningrove. This museum occupies buildings connected with the former Loftus Ironstone Mines on the coast between Saltburn and Staithes, and tells the story of ironstone mining. Visitors see part of the mine itself, as well as many interesting exhibits in the museum.

WHITBY MUSEUM, Pannett Park, Whitby. This remarkable museum covers every imaginable local subject, including geology, archaeology, zoology, history and, of particular interest, the story of Whitby shipping, with features on the famous whaling captain, William Scoresby, and of course the great explorer James Cook. The museum's fossil collection is of special note. And even if none of the above is your particular interest, you should still visit Whitby Museum simply for itself - for it is a near-perfect Victorian 'period piece', founded in 1823 and hardly altered since.

WOOD END MUSEUM, The Crescent, Scarborough. This fine Georgian building, set in charming gardens, was once the home of the Sitwell family, to whom two rooms are devoted. The rest of the museum is largely based on a natural history theme, with an aquarium, conservatory and other most attractive displays.

ZETLAND LIFEBOAT MUSEUM, Redcar. The Zetland lifeboat is the oldest surviving lifeboat in the world, dating from 1800. The fact that she saw 78 years' service and saved over 500 lives is a tribute both to Henry Greathead, the craftsman who built her, and to the brave men who served in her. Her story is one of incomparable heroism and will enthral any visitor.

Some Towns & Villages of the Area

Some towns and villages in this list are well-known: Goathland, Helmsley, Hutton-le-Hole, Lealholm and Staithes have long been favourites with visitors. However, we hope that this chapter can suggest new places to explore.

AISLABY On the slopes of the Esk Valley near Whitby, Aislaby's stone-built houses were home to the quarrymen who provided the famous building stone. Around the village are many medieval packhorse routes, and Featherbed Lane, leading to Sleights, is reputedly Britain's narrowest King's Highway.

AYTON is divided into East and West Ayton by the River Derwent, the bridge over which was built in 1775 with stone from C14th Ayton Castle. East Ayton church dates from Norman times.

BOULBY A tiny settlement on the highest point of the coast. Boulby Cliff is said to be the burial place of the great Norse poet and chieftain, Beowulf. Boulby is thought to be a corruption of his name. No remains have been found, but he could not have chosen a more magnificent resting place.

BRANSDALE A hamlet at the head of the valley of the same name. Much land belongs to the National Trust. Interesting gravestones in the churchyard.

CASTLETON An important stop on the Esk Valley railway, this village saw a mining boom in C19th. The 'motte' of the C11th castle survives.

COMMONDALE A small hamlet in the valley of the Sleddale Beck. Many C19th buildings are built with the products of the local brick and ceramic works.

COXWOLD A delightful Dales village with many historic features, not least Shandy Hall, home of Laurence Sterne (see 'Famous People') and Newburgh Priory (see 'Halls and Gardens').

DANBY An interesting village in the Esk Valley, where the author Canon Atkinson (see 'Famous People') was vicar. Danby Castle (see 'Castles'), built by the Latimers, was for a time home to Catherine Parr, Henry VIII's last wife. For information on the National Park, visit the Moors Centre here.

EBBERSTON An attractive village with a Norman church and charming C18th Hall, sometimes open to the public. Renowned water gardens.

EGTON on the north of the River Esk, and Egton Bridge to the South both enjoy fine views. There is known to have been a Roman Camp nearby.

FARNDALE This small valley, now a nature reserve, is famous for its wild daffodils. In spring, a one-way road system operates.

FILEY A traditional seaside town with the famous headland Filey Brigg, and good coastal walks, including 'Century Way' from Filey to York. There is also a C12th church, an interesting Folk Museum in Queen Street, and the Annual Edwardian Festival.

GOATHLAND A well-known and captivating village, also a halt on the Esk Valley Railway. The 'Abbot's House' of 1779 marks a former hermitage, from whose humble beginnings the village developed. Is Goathland the only English village that ever had a golf course passing through its very centre? A 6-hole course was founded in 1890, converted to 9 holes in 1895, and closed in the 1940s. Ideal walking along the Ellerbeck and Murk Esk to such beauty spots as Mallyan Spout and Water Ark. Has an interesting Heritage Centre.

GOLDSBOROUGH is the site of a Roman signal station discovered in 1918 between Staithes and Whitby. The defensive earthworks include a deep outer ditch.

GREAT AYTON This picturesque village beside the River Leven is associated with Captain Cook. The Church of All Saints has much Norman masonry.

GUISBOROUGH Once the capital of County Cleveland, now a dormitory town with an attractive market centre. The ruins of Guisborough Priory, founded by Robert de Brus in 1119, are impressive. At Tocketts Mill is a renovated working waterwheel.

HARWOOD DALE Small village in open country near Broxa Forest; the start of the Forestry Commission Long Distance Walk finishing at Allerston. Church of 1892. Ruined Jacobean chapel of 1634 lies on private land.

HAWNBY Nestles in an attractive setting under the Hambleton Hills in the Rye Valley. Arden Hall (not open) is built on the site of a C12th Benedictine nunnery. Pleasant walks nearby.

HAWSKER A village between Whitby and Robin Hood's Bay which boasts a pre-Norman Conquest stone cross.

HELMSLEY See special feature.

HINDERWELL by the main Saltburn to Whitby road, is named after St Hilda's Holy Well, of which remains are found in the churchyard. This well was blessed by St Hilda 1300 years ago.

HUTTON-LE-HOLE One of Yorkshire's most lovely and celebrated villages. Don't miss Ryedale Folk Museum (see 'Museums and Galleries').

INGLEBY GREENHOW On the northern edge of the Cleveland Hills, this village has a Norman church much altered in the C18th but retaining some good stone carving. High on Ingleby Moor is Burton Howe, four vast Bronze Age cairns.

The pretty village of Lockton

KILBURN A tidy village below the famous 'White Horse' described in Walk 4. There is a ½ mile waymarked 'White Horse Walk'. Kilburn was the home of woodcarver Robert Thompson (the Mouseman), some of whose work is in the ancient village church. His grandsons have succeeded him, and a host of other workshops now flourish nearby. The Kilburn Feast, an annual four day sporting event, is also famous.

KILDALE This pretty village in the River Leven valley once had a moated castle belonging to the Percy family. Fine stained glass in church. The site of the Cistercian nunnery, Baysdale Abbey, now occupied by a farmhouse, is 2 miles away.

KIRKBYMOORSIDE A small, hillside market town, where George Villiers, 2nd Duke of Buckingham, died after a hunting accident, in a house now named Buckingham House. The remains of a Norman castle are barely visible on nearby Viviers Hill.

KIRKDALE, near Kirkbymoorside. Famous for Kirkdale Cave (see page 12), and St Gregory's Minster, a tiny secluded church in a beautiful setting.

KIRKLEATHAM A village of great architectural distinction, south of Redcar, with magnificent almshouses.

LASTINGHAM A beautiful, ancient village lying snug between Rosedale and Farndale. The remains of its Norman Church are exceptional.

LEALHOLM A gem nestling in the sheltered valley of the River Esk, which winds its way through the village after cascading down Crunkley Ghyll. Cross by the picturesque stone road-bridge or by a series of sturdy stepping stones. John Costello, local stonemason and dialect poet known as Bard of the Dales, who became a renowned Methodist preacher, lived here in the C19th.

LITTLEBECK A small hamlet in the valley of the Little Beck, near the Falling Foss waterfall.

LIVERTON Fine Norman architecture in the church. To the east are the ruins of Handale Priory, a Cistercian nunnery.

LOCKTON A dispersed settlement near the Hole of Horcum, and the Whitby to Pickering road, with a C13th church.

LYTHE enjoys fine coastal views from the top of Lythe Bank near Whitby. The church of St Oswald, built in 1910 on a C12th foundation, contains fine Anglo-Saxon stone cross remains. Nearby is Mulgrave Castle (not open), dating from 1735. In the grounds are the remains of two earlier castles.

MIDDLESBROUGH is the busy urban creation of the Industrial Revolution, before which it was an insignificant hamlet. A splendid industrial landmark from those days is the Transporter Bridge. With the Cleveland Centre and the surrounding shopping streets, the town offers excellent shopping and opportunities for leisure pursuits. It contains the Dorman Museum of local history, the Middlesbrough Art Gallery, the Cleveland Art Gallery, and the Cleveland Crafts Centre. Nearby are Newham Grange Leisure Farm at Coulby Newham, the Captain Cook Birthplace Museum (see 'Museums and Galleries') and the beautiful National Trust property, Ormesby Hall. Sports enthusiasts will enjoy Tennis World at Marton, where important tournaments are staged.

The interesting Captain Cook Birthplace Museum

NORTHALLERTON Anglo-Saxon in origin,

the market town's heyday was in the coaching era of the C18th and C19th. It still has many houses and inns of that period. The Battle of the Standard was fought three miles north in 1138 between the English and Scots. 12,000 Scotsmen died. A Scottish raid in 1318 almost destroyed the town by fire.

OSMOTHERLEY Large, attractive village on the western slopes of the moors. Nearby lie C13th Mount Grace Priory and the C16th Lady's Chapel. Osmotherley is on the ancient Hambleton Drove Road and the more recent Cleveland Way, while the Lyke Wake Walk (see page 31) starts to the north. A stone cross and market stall mark the village centre beside a very early Methodist chapel, dated 1754.

PICKERING See special feature.

RAVENSCAR On the cliffs at the southern end of Robin Hood's Bay, it marks the end of the 40-mile Lyke Wake walk (see page 31) and has a National Trust Centre with marine aquarium and wildlife displays. There are fine nature trails and walks of interest to geologists. A viewing panel allows observation of one former alum works, and there are remains of others to be seen. The site of a Roman signal station is nearby.

ROBIN HOOD'S BAY See special feature.

Descending into the beauties of Rosedale

ROSEDALE ABBEY A village built partly from the ruins of a nearby abbey. A major centre for iron ore mining in the C19th and early C20th, and a good base for walking. The Milburn Arms Hotel overlooking the village green is an ideal place to unwind and sample fine food and wines.

RUNSWICK Coastal village with a fine bay.

SALTBURN Unspoilt Victorian seaside resort.

SANDSEND Where the long expanse of sand from Whitby ends. The two villages, of Sandsend and East Row, are stream-side sites, where waters emerge from Mulgrave Woods. The ruins of Mulgrave Castle are nearby.

SCARBOROUGH See special feature.

SCAWTON An old village near Helmsley. The church was established by the monks of Bylands Abbey, from where the church bell, one of the oldest in England, is taken. The local inn used to be the smallest in Yorkshire.

STAITHES See special feature.

SWAINBY Farmhand Harry Cooper, reputedly the tallest man in the world at 8ft 6ins, who featured in Barnum's Colossal Show in the USA, lived here.

THIRSK See special feature.

The picturesque village of Thornton-le-Dale

THORNTON-LE-DALE is an ancient and attractive village east of Pickering, a favourite with visitors. C14th church; almshouses dated 1657; and the famous 'Thatched Cottage'.

UGTHORPE A small moorland village south of Staithes, once in turmoil when the Catholic Church was being persecuted. Father Postgate was executed at York for saying Mass here.

WESTERDALE The former shooting lodge of Westerdale Hall now acts as youth hostel. Look for the medieval bow bridge, restored in 1870.

WHARRAM PERCY This 'lost' medieval village near Malton was re-excavated in 1990.

WHITBY See special feature.

WHORLTON A once-important village on the north west edge of the moors. Now there is only an interesting church, a farm, and the ruins of the castle built in the reign of Richard II. The conical hill above the village is Whorl Hill.

TICs & Useful Information

Tourist Information Centres

DALBY FOREST VISITOR CENTRE
(April-end October)
Low Dalby, Pickering, YO18 7LT
Tel: 01751 460295
FILEY
(May to September daily, weekends rest of year)
Town Hall, John Street, YO14 9DW
Tel: 01723 512204
GREAT AYTON
(March-October daily, closed off season)
High Green Car Park, Cleveland, TS9 6BJ
Tel: 01642 722835
GUISBOROUGH
Priory Grounds, Church Street,
Cleveland, TS14 6HL
Tel: 01287 633801
HELMSLEY
(Daily in summer, weekends off-season)
Market Place, YO6 5BL
Tel: 01439 770173
HUTTON-LE-HOLE
(March-October daily, closed off season)
Ryedale Folk Museum,
Hutton-le-Hole, YO6 6UA
Tel: 01751 417367
MALTON
58 Market Place, YO17 0LW
Tel: 01653 600 048
MIDDLESBROUGH
51 Corporation Road, Cleveland, TS1 1LT
Tel: 01642 243425/264330
MOORS CENTRE
(April to October daily, weekends off-season)
Lodge Lane, Danby,
Whitby, YO21 2NB
Tel: 01287 660654
NORTHALLERTON
The Applegarth Car Park,
North Yorkshire, DL7 8LZ
Tel: 01609 776864
PICKERING
Eastgate Car Park, YO18 7DU
Tel: 01751 473791
REDCAR & CLEVELAND BOROUGH COUNCIL
3 Dundas Street, TS10 3AD.
Tel: 01642 471921
SALTBURN
3 Station Buildings, TS12 1AQ
Tel: 01287 622422
SCARBOROUGH
St Nicholas Cliff,
North Yorkshire, YO11 2EP
Tel: 01723 373333

THE NORTH YORK MOORS NATIONAL PARK SUTTON BANK VISITOR CENTRE
(Easter-end October daily,
weekends off-season)
Sutton Bank, Thirsk, YO7 2EK
Tel: 01845 597426
THIRSK
(Easter-1st October daily,
closed off-season)
16 Kirkgate, YO7 1PQ.
Tel: 01845 522755
WHITBY
New Quay Road, YO21 1DH
Tel: 01947 602674

Other Useful Addresses

THE FORESTRY COMMISSION
231 Corstorphime Road,
Edinburgh EH12 7AT
Tel: 01313 340303
NATIONAL TRUST COASTAL CENTRE
(April-September)
Ravenscar, Scarborough, YO13 0NE
Tel: 01723 870138
NORTH YORK MOORS NATIONAL PARK
Bondgate, Helmsley, York, YO6 5BP
Tel: 01439 770657
NORTH YORKSHIRE MOORS ASSOCIATION
Mr Derek Statham, The Boot Garth,
Maunby, nr Thirsk, YO7 4HG
Tel: 01845 587308
THE COUNCIL FOR NATIONAL PARKS
246 Lavender Hill, London, SW11 1LJ
Tel: 0171 9244077
COUNTRYSIDE COMMISSION
Warwick House, Grantham Road,
Newcastle-upon-Tyne, NE2 1QF
Tel: 0191 2328252
RAMBLERS ASSOCIATION
Tel: 01642 474864

Coastguards

HUMBER M.R.S.C.
(Marine Rescue Sub-Centre)
Tel: 01262 672317
TYNE-TEES M.R.S.C.
(Marine Rescue Sub-Centre)
Tel: 0191 2572691

Fell Rescue Services

EMERGENCY SERVICES
Tel: 999

Weather Forecasts

For a brief recorded summary
Tel: 0990 100 844
For detailed information
Tel: 0891 500 762 (Weathercall)

SOME ESSENTIAL SERVICES FOR THE VISITOR